ECONOMICS OF MENTAL ILLNESS

Joint Commission
on Mental Illness and Health

MONOGRAPH SERIES / NO. 2

Economics

of Mental Illness

RASHI FEIN

A REPORT TO THE STAFF DIRECTOR, JACK R. EWALT
1958

Basic Books, Inc., Publishers, New York

Foreword

THIS IS the second of a series of monographs to be published by the Joint Commission on Mental Illness and Health as part of a national mental health survey that will culminate in a final report containing findings and recommendations for a national mental health program.

The present document constitutes a report of the project director to the staff director of the Joint Commission.

Titles of the monograph series, together with the principal authors, are listed here in the approximate order of scheduled publication:

1. *Current Concepts of Positive Mental Health*
   Marie Jahoda, Ph.D.

2. *Economics of Mental Illness*
   Rashi Fein, Ph.D.

3. *Mental Health Manpower*
   George W. Albee, Ph.D.

4. *Nationwide Sampling Survey of People's Mental Health*
   Angus Campbell, Ph.D., and Gerald Gurin, Ph.D.

5. *The Role of Schools in Mental Health*
   Wesley Allinsmith, Ph.D., and George W. Goethals, Ed.D.

These monographs, each a part of an over-all study design, will contain the detailed information forming the basis of a final report. From the data in the individual studies and other relevant information, the headquarters staff will prepare a summary document incorporating its findings and recommendations for national and state mental health programs. This summary document will have the approval of the Joint Commission before its publication in the form of an official report.

This final report will be published by Basic Books and transmitted to the United States Congress, the Surgeon General of the Public Health Services, and the Governors of the States, together with their representatives in the public health and mental health professions, in accordance with the provisions of the Mental Health Study Act of 1955.

Participating organizations, members and officers of the

Joint Commission, as well as headquarters and project staffs, are listed in the pages immediately preceding this foreword.

The Joint Commission, it may be seen, is a nongovernmental, multidisciplinary, nonprofit organization representing a variety of national agencies concerned with mental health. Its study was authorized by a unanimous resolution of Congress and is financed by grants from the National Institute of Mental Health and from private sources.

Additional copies of *Economics of Mental Illness* may be purchased from the publisher or from book dealers.

JOINT COMMISSION ON MENTAL ILLNESS AND HEALTH

Staff Review

ALL OF US who are concerned with mental health would like definitive answers to such questions as these:

How much does mental illness cost the people of the United States?

How much would it cost to provide the highest possible standard of care for the mentally ill?

Can we afford these costs? More exactly, which can we better afford—the cost in human misery caused by mental illness or the cost in dollars to provide the best care we know how to give?

Could greatly increased expenditures be justified from an economic as well as humanitarian viewpoint?

And, of course, the legislators would like to know—where is the money coming from?

We asked Rashi Fein, Ph.D., of the Department of Economics at the University of North Carolina and formerly staff member of the President's Commission on the Health Needs of the Nation, to examine such issues. We already knew that the data necessary to give all the answers about costs did not exist, but we believed an economist might be able to show us the routes to the information that would provide the answers.

We are satisfied that Dr. Fein has done so in the present monograph. The essential value of his study is to provide sound methods of computing the costs of mental illness. On this basis, his report should be of lasting value to any branch of federal or state government that would like to know how to develop reliable and meaningful cost figures as an aid to measuring the extent of the mental illness problem and progress toward its solution.

Economics of Mental Illness defines both direct costs and indirect costs: (1) Direct costs are actual expenditures for the care of the mentally ill by public and private agencies, by the patients or their families, and by public institutions and private foundations interested in mental health research. (2) Indirect costs are calculated on the basis of the annual loss of production, of annual earnings, and of work years by patients who are hospitalized and could be presumed to be, if they were not hospitalized, gainfully employed in a full-employment period.

Dr. Fein estimates the direct costs of mental illness to the American economy at more than $1.7 billion a year, but specifies that this is an understatement because certain known items of direct cost have not been reported. His figure includes the care of mental patients in all public mental hospitals and voluntary nonprofit and private mental hospitals; a minimum estimate of the cost of private psychiatric care; Veterans Administration pensions and compensation for psychiatric disabilities, and federal, state, and private foundation investments in mental health research.

The $1.7 billion does not include certain unavailable items such as capital construction and depreciation (it is impossible accurately to assess these costs in any given year because of varying practices among various states in computing depreciation and in financing public bonds for construction). Other omitted items are listed in Chapter I.

The direct-cost total includes an estimate of $100 million as the probable minimum direct cost of private psychiatric care, based on the gross income of psychiatrists in full-time private practice. The total does not, however, include payments to psychiatrists in part-time practice, to general practitioners, or to internists for care of patients with mental illness, inasmuch as the data from these sources is too fragmentary.

In the absence of data on what percentage of G.P. income is derived from patients whose complaints are primarily psychological, Dr. Fein conjectures this cost as being in the range of $206 million (10 per cent) to $1.03 billion (50 per cent). The similar item for specialists in internal medicine is in the range of $35 million (low estimate) and $175 million (high estimate).

Thus, including private psychiatric care as well as private general and specialized medical care of the mentally ill, the conjectural range of this direct-cost item is from $341,-000,000 (low estimate) to $1,305,000,000 (high estimate).

If these general practice and internal medicine items, based on unsatisfactory data, were combined with the more reliable figure of $1.7 billion, the total direct costs of mental illness would then lie in the range of $1.941 billion to $2.9 billion a year.

The annual cost of public mental hospital care alone (not including VA hospitals) is more than $660 million for the year cited. This represents an expenditure of $3.26 per patient per day.

If this expenditure were raised to ten dollars a day, considered by the American Psychiatric Association as the amount needed for a minimum standard of adequate hospital care, this figure alone would approach $2 billion.

Dr. Fein estimates the indirect losses for patients resident in public mental institutions for one year to be $700 million. Indirect losses for patients in federal mental institutions, such as VA mental hospitals, are excluded from this computation.

Dr. Fein places the present value of all potential future earnings of patients constituting annual first admissions to public mental hospitals at $1.9 billion. Based on probable death and discharge rates, the present value of the losses would be about $800 million, representing 556,000 labor-force years.

The greatest indirect loss occurred in the age group 25 to 34.

The annual direct and indirect costs of mental illness therefore can be estimated *at the very minimum* to be upwards of $2.4 billion—$1.7 billion plus $700 million.

The above total does not include private medical costs other than private psychiatric care. Judging from Dr. Fein's discussion of low and high estimates of this item, with due allowance for the fragmentary nature of information in this direction and with full knowledge that omitted categories of costs cannot be estimated, the total direct and indirect cost of mental illness in the United States may be safely assumed to be in excess of $3 billion a year.

In the process of developing the above estimates, Dr. Fein has devised a method enabling any State or the United States to estimate direct costs in relation to: age of patient upon admission to a hospital, diagnosis, and length of hospitalization. He calculates the indirect costs in lost work years due to illness-absenteeisms for various diagnostic categories.

He discusses the differences between estimates in this study and some others that have been published, advising caution in comparing published data on costs because of the absence of standardization among the reporting agencies. Some fail to give the basis of computation, and others use different bases.

He warns against an economic approach that holds large direct costs as undesirable and something to be eliminated, pointing out that the primary purpose of nonprofit institutions is not to make a profit but to provide service and that, even in profit-making enterprises, costs need be minimized only to what is consistent with a given level of production.

In determining what should and can be spent for mental illness out of existing resources, he recommends that the following economic reasoning is appropriate:

Costs cannot be eliminated. The only meaningful concept is that total costs comprise both direct and indirect costs. The nation bears the cost of mental illness whether it finances the direct costs or not. Economic considerations do not necessarily concern themselves with human or ethical values, but it is possible that increases in direct costs may reduce total costs. Measures reducing indirect costs are welcome, even though they may add to direct costs.

To illustrate, Dr. Fein cites statistics for a six-state reporting group showing that 100 patients admitted to state hospitals for the first time with schizophrenia require 71 patient years of care in the first year. By increasing direct expenditures aimed at treatment and discharge, Massachusetts state hospitals have reduced this patient-year requirement in the first year of hospitalization to 53 per 100. Costs are proportional to success.

Dr. Fein refrains from attempting to tell legislators where to find the money to meet the needs of mental illness as well as all other public needs, but suggests that an economy can afford to spend whatever it desires to spend. All that is necessary to spend more on one thing is to spend less on something else. What will be spent depends on the tax rate and the value system we embrace. The public and its leaders must make the choice.

This study has furnished some of the information on which policy decisions may be based. As already indicated, it also provides an outline of a method to be used in further research in the economics of mental illness.

Unanswered questions can only be answered through continued research.

JACK R. EWALT, M.D., *Director*

Contents

[xv]

List of Tables

ECONOMICS OF MENTAL ILLNESS

I

Introduction

THE ECONOMICS of mental illness is a broad area that includes a variety of interesting topics. The boundaries of the field are hazy and may be drawn wider or narrower. On the one hand, it can overlap into questions usually considered as falling in the sociological domain; on the other hand, it can include epidemiological research. In this study we shall limit ourselves to a subject which lies in the area traditionally reserved for economics, the subject of costs. The investigation will be concerned with the costs of mental illness and their implications. Although necessarily we shall allude to subjects outside this specific area, our chief interest will lie in the problem of costs—their meaning and their measurement.

It is certainly not necessary to justify the importance of such an investigation. Even without undertaking intensive study of the economics of mental illness we all know that it is an expensive malady. In 1953, the Committee on Interstate and Foreign Commerce of the House of Representatives conducted a health inquiry on "the causes, control, and remedies of the principal diseases of mankind." Mental illness was one of the diseases investigated. All of the following remarks are taken from the printed record of these hearings.

Mental illness is the Nation's No. 1 health problem.

More than half of all hospital beds in this country are occupied by the mentally ill.

The number of mentally ill patients in the United States exceeds the number of patients suffering from any other type of illness.

Mental ill health represents our greatest health problem in cost.

Conservative estimates based on incidence studies have shown that approximately 50 per cent of patients who are treated in general practice have psychiatric complications.

If the present birth rate remains constant, if the number of mentally ill who are hospitalized remains constant, and if the cost for hospitalizing the mentally ill remains constant, each year's crop of new babies will, because of the percentage of them who will go to mental hospitals, cost the taxpayers—this is just the taxpayer and not any private foundation—$800 million before they die.

At least 6 per cent of the total population, 9,000,000 people, suffer from a serious mental disorder.

Of 980,000 disability discharges from the Army during the period December 1941 through December 1945, 43 per cent were for neuropsychiatric reasons.

Of the 500,000 resident patients in our State mental hospitals, one-quarter have been hospitalized for more than 16 years, one-half for more than 8 years, and three-fourths for more than 2.5 years (Committee on Interstate and Foreign Commerce, 1953, pp. 1030–1134).

Additional data and documentation of the importance of mental illness are available in a variety of sources ranging from the professional journals to published documents by various government bureaus and commissions and pamphlet material of voluntary health associations. But to provide further evidence that mental health is a problem worth worrying about is certainly unnecessary. Everyone is already aware, if even in a rough way, of the dimensions of this problem in terms of human suffering and drain on manpower. The body of this report (in particular Chapters III and IV on direct and indirect costs) provides ample documentation of the significant *cost* aspects of mental illness.

The focus of our interest, as already indicated, will be the economic costs of mental illness. We shall be concerned both with expenditures and with loss in production (earning power). There have, of course, been numerous references to costs in the literature, and data on direct or indirect costs are often cited. We shall refer to some of the figures developed by the National Institute of Mental Health, the National Committee Against Mental Illness, Inc., the President's Commission on the Health Needs of the Nation, Benjamin Malzberg, and others. This study will attempt to probe more deeply and extensively than did earlier studies that were concerned primarily with one or another facet of costs. Although we shall, in many cases, use basic data developed by others, we shall pull together the available statistics, develop new data which are more current and more detailed, and make a particular effort to explain the methods we are using in order that our results be easily adjusted as even more current data become available. Our method and approach will differ from that of earlier authors in a number of important respects. These differences will be reflected in the final cost figures arrived at. We shall make our assumptions as explicit as possible and shall indicate the differences in method as we develop our data in the body of the report.

In embarking on a study of mental illness, we are immediately confronted with the problem of definition. What exactly shall we measure? What shall we exclude, what shall we include? Mental illness and mental health mean different things to different people. We have been forced to exclude certain problems because of the limitation of time and, in some cases, because of unavailability of data. Our figures will underestimate the costs of mental illness since we have not included the costs of mentally ill persons not under care; of drug addiction and alchoholism (except where patients were in public mental hospitals), of juvenile delinquency, mental deficiency, the mentally ill in public institutions other than mental; of police, court, penal, and social welfare agencies related to the mentally ill, and possibly of other factors. Our basis for inclusion and exclusion was largely pragmatic. The two important considerations governing our decisions were: time and availability of data.

The methods used to analyze any of the groups that we failed to cover would be the same as those used in Chapters III and IV in this study. If broader definitions of mental illness are desired, or if additional statistics become available, our data could be adjusted by applying the techniques utilized herein to the new information.

Most of our statistics will, therefore, deal with those people suffering from mental illness who are hospitalized. This is the bulk of the *measurable* problem and it is in this area that the best data are found. In many cases, of course, we have faced the "normal" problem that arises when one works with statistical data: the information is gathered and published by various agencies for their own purposes and subsequently must be used by others for entirely different purposes. We have "reconstructed" original data and adapted it to make it useful to us. Where this could not be done, i.e., where data would not yield the necessary information, interesting questions had to remain unanswered. We feel, however, that the computations presented in the four statistical chapters of this study (Chapters III-VI) will be useful to the reader not only in terms of the statistics they yield and the methods they illustrate but also because they show how data in this field can be "adapted" to new purposes.

OUTLINE OF STUDY

In order to provide a map for the reader to follow, we shall indicate briefly the general form of the report. The verbal chapters are probably self-explanatory and we shall, therefore, outline the statistical sections in somewhat more detail. The reader will also find summaries at the conclusion of Chapters III-VI. It is hoped that these will be of assistance.

Chapter II: In this section we set forth some definitions of costs (direct and indirect). We attempt to provide a rationale for our measurement of indirect costs and indicate the philosophical foundation for our measurements. The concepts set forth in this section are utilized in the rest of the report. This, then, is the explanation of our broad approach.

Chapter III: In this section we develop data on direct costs (expenditures). We include State, Federal, and private research expenditures. Tentative estimates are made of parts of the private costs of care for the mentally ill.

Chapter IV: Here we deal with indirect costs (loss of production, earnings, or work years). We calculate the annual loss for those patients resident in public institutions. This is expressed in work years and in dollars. We then compute the losses due to prolonged illness-absenteeism. These are also calculated on an annual basis. Shifting our emphasis from the costs in a given year, we then analyze the future losses over a period of time (discounted to their present value) for all first admissions. These are computed on two bases: (1) The assumption that patients who enter the hospital never leave; (2) The assumption that patients are discharged. These losses are calculated for hypothetical populations and for actual admissions in 1954.

Chapter V: In this chapter we first analyze the years of care required for a hypothetical group of first admissions with a given age and sex distribution. This analysis provides information on costs as a function of age at admission. We then use a similar analysis to estimate the cost of care for the period 1954-1959 for those patients first admitted to public prolonged care hospitals in 1954. Data on the costs of various mental disorders are also provided.

Chapter VI: We compute the expected total working years for each diagnostic category. This is a function of the number in each category admitted to mental institutions and of their age distribution. We are then able to assess the relative economic significance of various mental disorders. We apply estimates of expected working time *lost* to the data already derived. This permits us to recognize that, with today's knowledge, certain mental disorders are "more severe" than others. These calculations can be used to judge the economic burden caused by the admissions in the various diagnostic categories. Data on prolonged illness-absenteeism losses caused by various disabilities are also provided.

Chapter VII: In our concluding remarks we discuss the implications of our results, their meaning and significance.

II

The Concept of Costs

To THE ECONOMIST the term "costs" is one that must be clearly defined. Almost any elementary economics text contains definitions for various types of costs: fixed, variable, average, total, average variable, average fixed, marginal, social, etc. The better the text (or should we say, the longer the text?), the more refinements appear and the more different definitions are presented. Although the different cost concepts are of vital importance in the examination and discussion of particular economic problems, it is fortunately not necessary that we wander down every highway and byway of costs in this study.

It may be noted that many of the economist's cost definitions and approaches would be useful to those noneconomists engaged in other fields of interest. Thus, for example, one often hears the statement that, since the cost per patient year in public mental hospitals is about $1200, an additional patient will "cost" $1200. Conversely, an "extra" discharge will "save" $1200. The economist's concept of the "margin" and of fixed, as opposed to variable, costs would be useful, indeed, in this area. Dividing total costs by total patient years tells us *nothing* about the costs incurred if an extra patient is admitted to the hospital or about the savings derived if an extra patient is discharged. It should be manifestly clear that certain expenditures included in the $1200 figure remain fixed regardless of small, and often, unfortunately, even of large, changes in numbers of patients, e.g., electricity, heat, water, psychiatric care, and nursing care, among others. Does an extra guest cost anything or does the hostess add more water to the soup? This is a vivid illustration of the difference between average and marginal costs, a difference that should always be remembered.

To the economist, then, it is virtually second nature to be explicit as to the "costs" that he is measuring. We shall, therefore, attempt to define carefully the concepts used in this study and thus make it possible for the reader better to follow the ensuing discussion.

Our concern will be with the direct and the indirect costs of mental illness. By direct costs, we mean the actual dollar expenditures on mental illness. We include the amount spent by government (local, State, and Federal), by philanthropic organizations, and by individuals on the care, cure, and prevention of mental illness. Although it may be argued that one should also include the dollar expenditures on "positive mental health," it is not necessary to debate this issue at this time. Our present purpose is that of distinguishing between direct and indirect costs.

The concept of indirect costs is a somewhat vague one. By *indirect* costs of mental illness, we mean the economic loss in dollars (or in work years) that society incurs because a part of society is suffering from mental illness. Thus, we are concerned with a "what would have been" approach—e.g., what would the individuals suffering from mental illness have added and contributed to our economy if they had not been ill? Although some might argue that such considerations are irrelevant—on the grounds, for example, that the contributions of a tormented van Gogh are greater than would be the contributions of an imaginary, mentally healthy van Gogh—we shall confess at the outset that our approach views mental illness as an undesirable occurrence. This view is basic to the study and we shall make no attempt to sell the merit of our position to the reader who feels that mental illness is "good." Even those who believe that mental illness results in a net gain to society would probably feel that there is a debit side to the ledger, but that the credit side outweighs the debit. We leave to them the problem of computing the credits, the "pluses." We present only the debits, the "minuses."

Having suggested the distinction between direct and indirect costs, we are now able to discuss the problems of measuring these items. At this stage, we shall limit ourselves to the conceptual problems encountered in such measurements. These problems are the same whatever one is discussing, be it mental illness, cancer, automobile accidents, or something else. In subsequent chapters, the study will suggest the special problems (e.g., inadequacy of data and poor definitions of the categories of expenditures) encountered when we apply our concepts to mental illness.

Although it may be difficult, in the real world, to obtain sufficient data on direct costs (expenditures) to feel comfortable about the dollar total arrived at, it is certainly not difficult to know the types of data one is seeking and, in most cases, something about the reliability of the data one obtains. The problems that are encountered exist on the definitional level—i.e., should this or that particular item be included as part of the cost (expenditures) of this disease (many of these questions of definition are also encountered when one attempts to measure indirect costs). Thus, some would suggest that the expenses associated with the operation of our penal institutions should be charged to the cost of mental illness, others would add in the cost of operating divorce courts, still others would include the cost of war (and presumably, though it is really a transfer payment, the interest on the national debt, since the latter was chiefly incurred as the result of war), and so on. It may be difficult to reach agreement, but once we have agreed on the set of definitions to be used, the remaining difficulties are of a statistical rather than philosophical nature.

In the case of indirect costs the problems are at once similar and different. To be sure, the definitional problems encountered above once again confront us. Having "solved" these problems once and having agreed on a set of definitions, it is not particularly difficult to "solve" them anew. These, however, are not the really troublesome questions. The important questions concern the basic assumptions that are implied by the technique used in measuring indirect costs. It is clear that, if we suggest that the society loses something when an individual is mentally ill, we imply not only that the individual fails to operate at his maximum capacity but that society could and would utilize him at his maximum if he could operate there. Put very simply, we imply: (1) that the individual could produce more if he were well than if he were sick; (2) that society would be prepared to have him produce more rather than less.

At first glance it might seem that these two assumptions are both obvious and realistic—that they would always be true. Although this may be the case with the first (and we shall assume it is), it is not always so with the latter. Clearly, society is not always organized to permit its members to produce to their maximum capacity. This would be the case during depression periods, for example. At such times the indirect costs of mental illness decline because the alternatives are not "if the individual were not mentally ill he would produce more," but rather "if the individual were not mentally ill he would be unemployed." In the topsy-turvy world of depression economics, mental illness reduces *unemployment* rather than the *gross national product*. This suggests that underlying our discussion of indirect costs is an assumption that an economy can and will organize itself to assure full employment. Some, of course, might feel less optimistic on this score, but it does not appear to the author that to proceed on the assumption that we will maintain a sensible economic world rather than a topsy-turvy one is a completely unreasonable course. Over and beyond that point, it seems to the author that the proper approach must be to place the responsibility where it rightly belongs. Those charged with reducing mental illness should not take the easy way out by saying, "What's the difference? These individuals would be unemployed if they weren't sick." Let them assume full employment; if it is not achieved, we will know where the responsibility for that shortcoming lies.[1]

Thus, our concept of indirect costs (what would have been produced) is tied to full-employment considerations. In addition, our definition suggests that we are concerned with the loss to the economy rather than the cash loss to the individual and his family. This is of considerable importance in the measuring of indirect costs. The emphasis on society rather than on the family forces us to use a "gross value" rather than a "net value" measure. The cash value of an individual to his family is the value of his wages and salaries (net of taxes) minus the value of his consumption expenditures. From the family's economic point of view, the breadwinner is both a producer and a consumer. What he produces minus what he consumes gives us the net value referred to. Thus, if we want to know what the family loses when the breadwinner is killed in an accident, we must remember to subtract the breadwinner's expenditures (on himself) from his earnings (wages and salaries).[2] This may appear a rather coldhearted approach, for it implies that the family is "better off" if a retired parent (not producing, but consuming) dies. The reader must remember that our discussion is limited to values as expressed in dollars and that, as long as we do not measure "psychic values" and impute dollar values to them, as long as we limit ourselves to economic values—and we do so limit ourselves—the family is "better off" in dollars and cents.[3]

Even when it is agreed that we are interested in the *economic* value of a man (or woman) to society as opposed to the *cash* value of a man (or woman) to his (or her) family, there remain problems concerning the approach to be used.

It is conceptually rather easy to measure the money value of a man to his family. This problem has been assayed in the courts which deal with indemnity cases and in the statistical bureaus of life insurance companies. In the selling of insurance, the attempt is often made to convince the individual of the importance of insurance by indicating that at his present income he is "worth" so much or so much to his family. The degree of refinement of such data as insurance agents may bring to the question may often leave something to be desired; the concepts of gross and net worth to the family are nevertheless simple enough. The concept of economic value to society is, on the other hand, rather complex. Thus, Dublin and Lotka, who analyze the money value of a man, state explicitly that their concern is *not* with the value of the individual's productive services to society.

The problems of estimating losses to the community arising from defects, injuries, or death to individuals involves other difficulties aside from the mere matter of statistical machinery and technique in collecting data. There is a fundamental difficulty in principle involved in all attempts to estimate losses to the community. This difficulty arises out of the fact that every person in the industrial community is both a co-operative producer (and from this point of view an asset to his fellows) and a competitor (and, as such, a liability). If he is eliminated, there may be a certain loss of production, though this does not follow, so long as there is any unemployment and a reserve force of men ready to fill the gap; but whether there be such a loss of production or not, some person or persons who step in to fill the gap are usually gainers when a worker is eliminated either temporarily or permanently. To strike the true balance between the total losses and gains thus occasioned is a problem for which no available method presents itself. All estimates of losses to the community obtained by some elementary process of totaling losses to wage earners, immediate families, or the like, must be viewed with extreme reserve (Dublin and Lotka, 1946, pp. 86–87).

Although we agree with Dublin and Lotka that one should use extreme reserve in assessing such data, we shall nevertheless attempt to make estimates of the very things they indicate are difficult to estimate. We should state that the problem of gain on the part of those who move into the positions now vacated does not appear to us to be a real problem in the type of economy the United States has experienced in the postwar decade. In this period enough jobs existed to permit most individuals to operate at their maximum potential even without the "vacancies."

In an interesting article entitled "The Cost of Road Accidents," D. J. Reynolds attempts to compute social costs of road accidents in Great Britain. He states:

The occurrence of road accidents inflicts a burden on the community which may be considered in two parts.

(i) The pain, fear, and suffering imposed by the occurrence, or the risk of occurrence, of road accidents. These are considered of great importance in a society that values human life and human welfare.

(ii) The more concrete and ascertainable burdens in the form of the net loss of output of goods and services due to death and injury and the expenditure of resources necessary to make good the effects of accidents, e.g. medical expenses, vehicle repairs and costs of administration.

For a variety of reasons it is beyond the competence of the economist to assign objective values to the losses suffered under (i) and this paper is therefore confined to the estimation of the burdens listed under (ii). The estimates contained in this paper give, therefore, only the minimum values that can be placed on the consequence of road accidents and as such are not a complete guide to the policy to be adopted and the expenditure to be incurred on accident prevention (Reynolds, 1956, p. 393).

Having stated the problem and approaching it, as can be seen, from the same point of view as we are, Mr. Reynolds then proceeds (p. 397) to (1) calculate the expected working life of individuals in the various age groups; (2) multiply this result by the average annual output per person minus the average annual consumption per person; (3) multiply the result by the number of deaths in each age group; (4) discount the values obtained in step 3 to the present. (When we discount a future dollar sum to the present, we take into account the effect of the interest rate and calculate how many dollars would be needed today in order to yield a given number of dollars sometime in the future.) What we find of greatest interest in this approach is the method used in arriving at the average annual output per person. In effect, he divides the net domestic product at factor cost (meaning the value at market prices minus any indirect business tax, such as sales or excise; this cost is roughly equivalent to the American concept of National Income) by the number of individuals in the working force, to arrive at an estimate of the individual's share of the net domestic product.[4]

In a sense, this approach asserts that all of the national product (income) and, therefore, any gains in national product are attributable to labor rather than to some combination of joint factors of production, land, labor, capital, etc. Although it may, indeed, be true that if there were no labor there would be no product, it is equally true that if there were no capital there would be very little product. This problem is not a new one for the economist. It is an old friend—not even dressed in new clothes. What is required is a marginal concept, and viewed in that light, it would seem that we should follow the approach that is implied in the concept of "marginal productivity."

The marginal productivity theory suggests that the best measure of an individual's contribution, i.e., of his productivity, is his wage. Clearly, he would not be paid more than he is "worth" and, it can be shown, would not be paid less than he is "worth."[5] The average contribution to society is, therefore, given by the average wage. It might appear that what we are measuring is the loss in wages; we emphasize, however, that this is not the case. We are measuring the loss in production as given by the loss in wages.

The difference between what we call the "Reynolds approach" and the marginal productivity approach is a substantial one in dollar terms. The Reynolds approach would cause losses to society to run at much higher levels. The two methods cannot be compromised by splitting the difference between them. The choice of method must be made on the basis of economic philosophy.

Yet another important issue remains to be analyzed. After deriving an "average output per head" figure, Mr. Reynolds derives a "consumption per head" statistic. This statistic is obtained by dividing total consumption at factor cost by total population. We have already indicated how this figure is utilized. The subtraction of consumption from output is essentially the same approach utilized by Dublin and Lotka in adjusting their "gross" value to arrive at a "net" concept. In our data we shall not deduct consumption from output. The reasons for this, it seems to us, are fundamental and indicate our point of view about the individual. As such, they merit some discussion.

Certainly the net figure derived by Dublin and Lotka to indicate the money value of a man to his family is correct for their purposes. It is not at all apparent, however, that the net concept is the correct one when we deal with the economic value of a man to society. It is true that man consumes partly in order to maintain himself, and in this sense some of his consumption may be considered as gross investment to take care of depreciation; it is also true, however, that consumption is an end in itself and can be viewed as a final, rather than an intermediate, step in the creation of other products. The question involved concerns the purposes for which an economy exists.

It is clear that some part of consumption is absolutely necessary for mere maintenance. It is equally clear that man consumes more than this minimal amount. The extra that he consumes over and above the minimum is an end in itself and the maximization of this amount is one of the aims of the economic system. This is one of the measures of the richness of a society and is one of the bases on which we differentiate between the underdeveloped economy, in which people work hard in order to have the bare minimum, and the more productive American economy, in which we have much more than the bare minimum. Our standards of subsistence levels of income rise as time goes on, and this is as it should be. Assume a bachelor earns five thousand dollars a year in an economy without taxes. Assume, further, that his consumption expenditures per annum are five thousand dollars; savings, thus, are zero. Is this individual's net worth to society zero (five thousand produced minus five thousand consumed)? This would hardly seem to be the case. On the five thousand dollars income, the individual enjoys life, and it is for this purpose that the social economy exists.

We arrive at the same conclusion even if we view the problem in real rather than in monetary terms. What would society lose if the individual we are discussing should die? Society would lose the five thousand dollars worth of production even though it would also be true that there would no longer be the five thousand dollars of consumption.

Also lost would be the enjoyment that the individual derives from his consumption. It may be true that, at the margin, the disutility of work is balanced by the utility derived from the marginal income, but the total utility of the income exceeds the total disutility of labor. Although these enjoyments cannot be measured directly, the fact that we work to earn income beyond what is necessary to sustain life suggests that they do exist and cannot be ignored.

It is for these reasons, too, that we reject the suggestion that only that part of consumption necessary for maintenance should be deducted. To do so would be to view man as a machine. A machine must be oiled, repainted, and so on in order to function, and these maintenance expenditures are properly deducted before arriving at the net value of the machine. Man, however, is not a machine and has value in his own right. The further difficulty remains that we cannot really answer the question, "What part of consumption is necessary?" In physiologic terms this can probably be measured, and some monetary value assigned to it, although it is surely clear that all of us would differ on the meaning of the term "necessary" and that, for some, the minimal standard would be significantly higher than it would be for others. It is clear, however, that there are psychological and sociological factors at work which may far outweigh the physiologically necessary expenditures. What is necessary and sufficient for one person to maintain himself may not be sufficient for another individual. The executive would not only be unhappy living on a janitor's income but might be unable to function effectively as an executive on the janitor's income. That which we consider the minimum for one economy may be far greater than the minimum for another economy. Minima differ in different societies and in the same society at different times and in different stages of development.

We thus join with the United States Department of Commerce in viewing consumption as a final rather than intermediate product. This is also the point of view implied in studies on the economic value of an education. In such studies, it is found that more education yields higher incomes. These incomes are sufficiently higher to make education a worthwhile investment even though it requires expenditures of time and money. We are aware that higher incomes are associated with higher levels of consumption. Yet we do not deduct these consumption expenditures from the higher income in calculating the economic benefits of an education. We view consumption as a final goal, although in many cases the greater consumption is necessary to achieve the higher income. Our approach in this study is, therefore, "traditional" in a philosophic sense, although at variance with that used by various other authors.

We have indicated that we shall measure the indirect costs (i.e., the value of productive services that fail to be performed) by imputing the average wage and salary income earned by employed individuals to those who are unemployed because of mental illness. In so doing, we assume that those mentally ill would be "average" if they were well. It may be, of course, that this would overstate the income such individuals would receive were they not mentally ill, i.e., it is possible that mental illness tends to strike low-income individuals. Since we are not sure of the causal relationships involved (i.e., possibly low incomes result from a predisposition to mental illness), and since it would be easy, if further research brings more information to light concerning previous and future incomes and occupations of those mentally ill, to adjust our results by dividing by the appropriate factor, we shall proceed as indicated.

It would be incorrect, however, to impute the average earned income to each and every person suffering from mental illness. To do so would be to assume that all these individuals would be employed if they were well. This is clearly not the case with women and is also not true even in the case of men. The problems relating to females are complex and will, therefore, be discussed somewhat later; in the case of males the question is simpler.

Even under conditions of full employment, there is always some unemployment. This frictional unemployment results from the fact that some individuals are unemployed for relatively short periods of time while looking for work or changing jobs, among other things. Some part, a small part, of the labor force will, therefore, not be employed. In addition to those who are unemployed, some individuals do not enter the labor force, i.e., they are not in the category that is able to work, willing to work, and seeking work. Some voluntarily exclude themselves from the labor force (they simply choose not to work); others are unable to enter it (they may be sick, in prison, etc.). Since this means that less than 100 per cent of the male population (even of what we normally consider working age) is employed, some adjustment should be made before we assume that 100 per cent of the mentally ill males would work if they were not mentally ill. The adjustment is obvious and will be discussed more fully in subsequent chapters. We shall assume that the same percentage of mentally ill would be employed if they were well as is the case with the general population.

If 80 per cent of the male population in a particular age bracket works, then we shall assume that 80 per cent of the mentally ill males in that age bracket would work if they were well. To each person in that 80 per cent we shall impute the average earned income.

For females our procedure will be the same. We shall again be concerned only with those women who enter the labor force and who are employed. Clearly, the probability of a female being employed (as given by the percentage who are employed) is far less than for males. This means that we are concerned with those women whose productive services enter the money market and not with the value of productive services that are not paid for. The value of the housewife's services is, therefore, excluded; the value of the domestic servant's services is included.

This procedure tends to undervalue the total services performed by the female but can be defended on the grounds that it is money values in which we are interested. Furthermore, to impute money values to those services which do not enter the money market would raise as many questions as it answers. Where would we draw the line? We, all of us, perform many services for ourselves and others that could be purchased. Should we impute a money value to all these services—e.g., shining shoes, changing a fuse, mowing the lawn, baking a cake?

The National Income data collected by the Department of Commerce does not include an estimate of the value of the services performed by the housewife. We shall follow the same procedure. This will tend to make the money value of woman appear very low. This is indeed the case, and we would caution the reader that the estimates of the economic value of the female to society differ substantially from the value to the family. In this respect, we approach the problem somewhat differently than does Benjamin Malzberg (1950), who calculates expected working years for women largely as if they all work. For our purposes, we believe the adjustment we make is correct.[6]

Further measurement problems will be elaborated upon as the various statistics are analyzed in the subsequent chapters. These problems are largely computational in nature and do not, therefore, enter into our discussion at this point. In this section we have been concerned with the definition of direct and indirect costs and with the framework and meaning of these measures. We have attempted to provide an understanding of the approach we shall use and of the reasons why we include or exclude certain variables. We are now ready to turn to the statistics themselves.

III

Some Measures and Statistics
of Direct Costs

THAT THE TOTAL direct cost of mental illness to the American economy is large is not a strikingly new idea or statement. That the burden to the individual States is large is also not remarkably new. Both statements, though true, are in themselves insufficient. How great are the costs? How large is the burden? In this section, we shall draw upon available materials to attempt to arrive at answers to these questions. We shall also discuss the reliability, adequacy, and shortcomings of the data.

As we have already indicated in Chapter II, by "direct costs" we mean the dollar expenditures on mental illness and mental health. These expenditures may be made by various individuals, associations, or governments. In all cases, however, we refer to a dollar quantity that is actually expended and not to an imaginary loss which assumes something about what an individual would create or earn if he were well rather than sick.

Table 3.1—Total Maintenance Expenditures for Patients
in Public Mental Hospitals, by State and
Region, 1954–1956 [a]

| | YEAR | | |
	1956	1955	1954
UNITED STATES	$662,146,372	$616,867,670	$568,379,739
New England	58,889,100	56,274,234	52,154,420
Maine	3,424,602	3,184,342	3,026,097
New Hampshire	3,726,568	3,592,863	3,383,164
Vermont	1,516,693	1,387,096	1,322,564
Massachusetts	31,933,633	30,351,554	28,579,350
Rhode Island	3,304,549	3,164,190	2,761,080
Connecticut	14,983,055	14,594,189	13,082,165
Middle Atlantic	198,076,417	192,408,609	172,631,309
New York	121,677,784	119,069,924	110,510,931
New Jersey	31,216,016	28,389,142 [b]	23,748,680
Pennsylvania	45,182,617	44,949,543	38,371,698
East North Central	143,159,995	129,040,172	121,075,376
Ohio	33,347,711	29,468,688	26,548,533
Indiana	15,410,584	12,136,898	10,432,082
Illinois	41,161,600	38,201,998	36,107,369
Michigan	34,571,518	32,023,989 [b]	31,780,505
Wisconsin	18,668,582	17,208,599 [b]	16,206,887
West North Central	49,715,305	45,771,029	44,078,672
Minnesota	12,573,653	12,598,456	12,284,369
Iowa	6,873,078	6,273,756 [b, d]	6,970,038
Missouri	12,341,466	10,262,907	9,411,867
North Dakota	2,025,722	1,942,097	1,783,258
South Dakota	1,899,501	1,607,632	1,521,821
Nebraska	6,571,342	5,417,693	5,147,253
Kansas	7,430,543	7,668,488	6,960,066
South Atlantic	78,584,663	70,013,607	66,146,002
Delaware	2,581,394	1,810,960	1,732,100
Maryland	12,196,749	11,279,506 [b, c]	10,065,022
District of Columbia	14,327,083	13,634,554	13,133,142
Virginia	10,698,331	9,257,022	8,369,328
West Virginia	3,794,642	3,616,709	3,701,151
North Carolina	10,583,939	10,374,256	10,141,020
South Carolina	5,007,600	4,764,532	4,335,791
Georgia	11,956,268	8,494,743	8,209,147
Florida	7,438,657	6,781,325	6,459,301

	YEAR		
	1956	1955	1954
East South Central	20,824,724	18,879,465	16,608,786
Kentucky	5,661,448	5,026,936	4,547,564
Tennessee	5,569,175	4,992,914 [b]	3,850,464
Alabama	5,693,330	5,120,431	4,778,285
Mississippi	3,900,771	3,739,184	3,432,473
West South Central	30,297,893	30,589,701	28,398,278
Arkansas	4,703,446	4,528,186	4,628,130
Louisiana	6,268,343	5,480,297	4,762,205
Oklahoma	7,110,393	6,580,220	5,950,296
Texas	12,215,711	14,000,998	13,057,647
Mountain	17,701,061	16,096,379	14,951,394
Montana	2,138,411	1,829,976	1,800,898
Idaho	1,422,849	1,479,800	1,315,975
Wyoming	800,146	570,900 [b, e]	570,900
Colorado	7,861,325	6,690,811	6,304,230
New Mexico	1,582,646	1,378,817	1,306,446
Arizona	2,202,551	2,090,357	1,866,376
Utah	1,156,319	1,580,899	1,384,322
Nevada	536,814	474,819	402,247
Pacific	64,897,214	57,794,474	52,335,502
Washington	8,166,238	7,827,415	6,743,441
Oregon	5,341,377	5,141,288	4,833,817
California	51,389,599	44,825,771 [b, c]	40,758,244

[a] Figures include expenditures of state hospitals along with county hospitals in California, Iowa, Maryland, New Jersey, Tennessee and Wisconsin; for 1956, also, psychopathic hospitals in California, Colorado, Iowa, Massachusetts, Nebraska, New York, Ohio, and Tennessee.

[b] Figures taken from Public Health Reports, Vol. 71, No. 3, March 1956. They include psychopathic hospitals for those states which have them.

[c] Estimated by using data reported in the 1954 census of mental patients for those hospitals not supplying the special survey data for 1955 and using the 1955 survey data for those hospitals which did report.

[d] Estimated by applying, where required, the percentage change reported for similar data in the 1953 and 1954 census of mental patients to the 1954 figure since the hospitals in the state concerned did not supply the item requested.

[e] Estimated by using data reported for the 1954 census of mental patients since the hospitals in the state did not report in the special survey for 1955.

Source: Rearranged by region from Interstate Clearing House on Mental Health, Council of State Governments, Selected Tables on Resident Population, Finances and Personnel in State Mental Health Programs, 1956, Table 1. Footnotes in original source.

STATE EXPENDITURES

One of the best single sources of data on State expenditures on the mentally ill is the Interstate Clearing House on Mental Health, Council of State Governments. This organization gathers, summarizes, and publishes statistical material second to none in this field. Those doing research on mental illness should, indeed must, rely heavily on these data.

In 1956, the total maintenance expenditures, as reported by the Interstate Clearing House, for patients in public mental hospitals was $662,146,372. *Maintenance,* in this sense, refers to the care and treatment of patients and not to building construction or repair. This expenditure had grown 7.3 per cent from that in 1955, which in turn was 8.5 per cent greater than the 1954 expenditure. The rapid percentage growth was not, however, characteristic of every State, for, although most grew, others declined. The dollar expenditures are presented in Table 3.1.

These expenditures of about $660 million are, of course, only part of the annual State expenditures on mental illness and mental health. They are primarily the expenditures connected with the operation of the State, county, and psychopathic hospitals. They do, however, represent the major portion of State expenditures. In addition, the individual States spend (1955 data) about $13 million for mental health programs. This sum is apart from Federal grants-in-aid for the same programs. The State expenditures for these purposes are presented in Table 3.2.

The variation in State expenditures is, of course, striking. These variations are evident in both Tables 3.1 and 3.2. Although we would expect to find variation in such data, since

States vary in population, it is clear that the differences in State expenditures can hardly be accounted for by this factor alone. Nor can the differences be accounted for by the differences in the number of patients in mental institutions. If the latter were the case, the cost per patient day of care would be the same in all States. That such is not the case is shown in Table 3.3. The reader will note the variation from a low of $1.84 per patient day for Tennessee to a high of $5.51 for the District of Columbia and $4.74 for Connecticut. This difference may not appear impressive to some because of the relatively small figures involved. It is for this reason that we include the cost per patient year. These data, the reader will note, range from a low of $670.74 to highs of $2,012.23 and $1,728.55.

This is not the place to develop a theory, assuming even that such a theory could be developed, to explain such variations in expenditures. It should, however, be stated that part of these differences are "real"—that is, differences which cannot be explained by inadequacy of data, looseness of definition, or lack of comparability of items included and excluded. Although all these problems do exist, it is to be doubted that these factors alone could explain all the variations. It can further be argued that even if equal care were provided by the various States, there still would be differences in the costs of providing such care. These differences would exist because of regional or State differences in the cost of food, clothing, heat, etc., in the need for certain maintenance expenditures (fuel oil, snow shovels, or other items), and in the wages paid employees and the salaries paid medical staff members. All this is true; such differences do indeed exist. Yet a close look at Table 3.3 would indicate that these factors

Table 3.2—Estimated Expenditures for Mental Health, by State and Region, 1955

	For Mental Health Programs	Mental Health Programs and Maintenance in Public Mental Hospitals [a]
UNITED STATES	$13,377,656	$630,245,326
New England	979,641	57,253,875
Maine	51,075	3,235,417
New Hampshire	132,474	3,725,337
Vermont	42,117	1,429,213
Massachusetts	461,837	30,813,391
Rhode Island	124,852	3,289,042
Connecticut	167,286	14,761,475
Middle Atlantic	3,250,829	195,659,438
New York	1,565,773	120,635,697
New Jersey	436,047	28,825,189
Pennsylvania	1,249,009	46,198,552
East North Central	3,193,349	132,233,521
Ohio	923,391	30,392,079
Indiana	299,971	12,436,869
Illinois	1,501,432	39,703,430
Michigan	203,749	32,227,738
Wisconsin	264,806	17,473,405
West North Central	665,454	46,436,483
Minnesota	161,194	12,759,650
Iowa	192,469	6,466,225
Missouri	164,124	10,427,031
North Dakota	17,301	1,959,398
South Dakota	66,356	1,673,988
Nebraska	38,529	5,456,222
Kansas	25,481	7,693,969
South Atlantic	1,766,494	71,780,101
Delaware	74,491	1,885,451
Maryland	187,931	11,467,437
District of Columbia	177,731	13,812,285
Virginia	611,900	9,868,922
West Virginia	48,833	3,665,542
North Carolina	102,195	10,476,451
South Carolina	140,072	4,904,604
Georgia	231,407	8,726,150
Florida	191,934	6,973,259

	For Mental Health Programs	Mental Health Programs and Maintenance in Public Mental Hospitals [a]
East South Central	253,528	19,132,993
Kentucky	38,664	5,065,600
Tennessee	117,309	5,110,223
Alabama	65,991	5,186,422
Mississippi	31,564	3,770,748
West South Central	391,446	30,981,147
Arkansas	28,700	4,556,886
Louisiana	130,904	5,611,201
Oklahoma	24,471	6,604,691
Texas	207,371	14,208,369
Mountain	259,343	16,355,722
Montana	61,808	1,891,784
Idaho	10,636	1,496,436
Wyoming	7,368	578,268
Colorado	71,673	6,762,484
New Mexico	16,185	1,395,002
Arizona	38,261	2,128,618
Utah	42,730	1,623,629
Nevada	10,682	485,501
Pacific	2,617,572	60,412,046
Washington	105,094	7,932,509
Oregon	85,432	5,226,720
California	2,427,046	47,252,817

[a] From 1955 data in Table 3.1.

Source: Rearranged by region from Interstate Clearing House on Mental Health, Selected Tables, 1956, Table 4.

cannot explain the full differences. States with essentially the same price levels and climatic conditions still show differences in costs per patient day of care.

In addition to the fact that States vary in their expenditures on patient care and presumably, therefore, in the quality and/or quantity of care given, they also appear to differ in their standards for admission and discharge of patients. This

Table 3.3—Daily and Yearly Per Capita Maintenance Expenditures at Public Mental Hospitals, by State, 1956 [a]

MAINTENANCE EXPENDITURES

	Daily [b]	Yearly
UNITED STATES	$3.26	$1,190.32
Alabama	2.13	777.78
Arizona	3.61	1,318.89
Arkansas	2.60	948.85
California	3.81	1,388.83
Colorado	3.78	1,380.15
Connecticut	4.74	1,728.55
Delaware	4.08	1,489.55
District of Columbia	5.51	2,012.23
Florida	2.54	925.78
Georgia	2.79	1,018.59
Idaho	3.18	1,159.62
Illinois	2.95	1,078.21
Indiana	3.84	1,401.47
Iowa	3.64	1,329.67
Kansas	4.60	1,678.46
Kentucky	2.07	755.87
Louisiana	2.08	758.70
Maine	3.12	1,140.01
Maryland	3.46	1,261.43
Massachusetts	3.83	1,397.59
Michigan	4.33	1,581.50
Minnesota	3.01	1,100.06
Mississippi	2.04	746.13
Missouri	2.84	1,036.05
Montana	3.08	1,122.53
Nebraska	3.80	1,386.07
Nevada	3.30	1,203.62
New Hampshire	3.83	1,397.29
New Jersey	3.89	1,418.07
New Mexico	4.35	1,587.41
New York	3.44	1,257.42
North Carolina	2.93	1,070.17
North Dakota	2.89	1,053.42
Ohio	3.25	1,176.54
Oklahoma	2.47	900.39
Oregon	2.95	1,077.76
Pennsylvania	3.06	1,118.24
Rhode Island	2.65	967.94
South Carolina	2.24	819.17

MAINTENANCE EXPENDITURES

	Daily [b]	Yearly
South Dakota	3.24	1,184.23
Tennesee	1.84	670.74
Texas	2.07	756.39
Utah	2.43	887.43
Vermont	3.24	1,183.99
Virginia	2.63	960.87
Washington	3.10	1,131.53
West Virginia	1.90	691.70
Wisconsin	3.40	1,242.17
Wyoming	3.36	1,227.22

[a] Figures include state hospitals along with county hospitals in California, Iowa, Maryland, New Jersey, Tennessee, and Wisconsin, and psychopathic hospitals in California, Colorado, Iowa, Massachusetts, Nebraska, New York, Ohio, and Tennessee.

[b] Calculated on the basis of 356 days.

Source: Interstate Clearing House on Mental Health, Selected Tables, 1956, Tables 2 and 3.

factor would also contribute to the differences in total expenditures that we noted in Table 3.1. Although we are not suggesting that the same proportion of population would be mentally ill in each State, it is nevertheless true that the large State differences in mental hospital beds per 1000 population would suggest that factors other than differences in patient load would be at work (Ginzberg, 1953). Data on mental hospital beds are presented in Table 3.4.

The reader should note that the data presented in Table 3.4 are somewhat outdated and should, therefore, treat the absolute figures with some caution. The differences between States, however, rather than the actual number of beds per 1000 population in each State, are of significance for our purposes.

In addition to expenditures on mental health programs and on maintenance at public hospitals for the mentally ill, the individual States have appropriated significant sums for

Table 3.4—Number of Acceptable Beds and Total Number of Existing Beds Per 1,000 Population, by State and Region, June 1952

| | MENTAL BEDS | |
	Existing Acceptable	Total Existing
UNITED STATES	2.8	3.2
New England	4.0	4.1
Connecticut	4.0	4.0
Maine	2.8	2.8
Massachusetts	4.3	4.3
New Hampshire	4.4	4.4
Rhode Island	3.9	3.9
Vermont	3.3	4.8
Central Atlantic	3.6	4.1
Delaware	2.1	3.5
District of Columbia	6.6	6.8
Maryland	2.6	2.6
New Jersey	3.3	3.3
New York	4.4	5.1
Pennsylvania	3.3	3.6
West Virginia	1.4	1.9
Southeast	2.1	2.5
Alabama	1.1	1.1
Arkansas	1.4	2.3
Florida	2.2	2.2
Georgia	2.9	2.9
Kentucky	2.8	2.8
Louisiana	2.1	3.0
Mississippi	1.5	2.5
North Carolina	2.4	2.4
South Carolina	1.8	1.9
Tennessee	2.3	2.4
Virginia	2.0	3.4
Southwest	1.9	2.1
Arizona	1.3	2.1
New Mexico	1.5	1.7
Oklahoma	3.4	4.3
Texas	1.5	1.5
East North Central	2.2	3.1
Illinois	2.3	3.1
Indiana	2.4	3.0

MENTAL BEDS

	Existing Acceptable	Total Existing
Michigan	1.9	2.9
Ohio	2.5	2.8
Wisconsin	2.1	4.4
West North Central	2.8	3.0
Iowa	1.2	2.1
Kansas	2.7	2.7
Minnesota	3.1	3.3
Missouri	3.1	3.1
Nebraska	3.6	3.6
North Dakota	3.6	3.6
South Dakota	2.9	2.9
Rocky Mountain	2.7	3.1
Colorado	3.4	4.4
Idaho	2.1	2.1
Montana	3.3	3.3
Utah	1.5	1.5
Wyoming	2.5	2.5
Far West	3.1	3.5
California	3.3	3.7
Nevada	1.9	1.9
Oregon	2.7	2.7
Washington	2.6	2.9

Source: Building America's Health, Vol. III, Table 329.

construction of new mental hospitals and for the expansion and renovation of existing institutions. This type of expenditure is nonrecurring, and it would be extremely useful if some depreciation formula could be applied to indicate what proportion of the dollar capital expenditures in any given year should be charged to the expenses of that year.

Unless we allocate capital costs (via a depreciation formula) to various years rather than to the year in which the construction takes place (the same problem holds for durable equipment), we distort the meaning of our final figures. Expenditures would fluctuate every year depending on capital construction expenditures. They would be high in years when large expenditures were made and low when small expenditures were made.

This is a problem of which the business world is keenly aware. The availability and the nature of the data do not, unfortunately, permit us to depreciate capital equipment with any feeling of confidence in the results of our computation. The shortcomings of utilizing the expenditure data on capital investment of any one year and regarding that year as typical are so apparent that we shall present data on total investment in hospitals, before citing data on investment in any given year. This course will enable the reader to judge for himself the size of the relationships involved.

In 1947, the non-Federal psychiatric hospitals in the United States, numbering 499, had total assets of $965,549,000. The number of hospitals and their total assets increased in the following years. As can be seen in Table 3.5, there were 525 hopitals in 1956 with total assets of $2.3 billion.

Table 3.5—Number of Non-Federal Psychiatric Hospitals and Total Assets, 1946–1956

Year	Number of Hospitals	Total Assets [a] (000 omitted)
1946	476	$ [b]
1947	499	965,549
1948	504	1,143,078
1949	507	1,260,963
1950	533	1,440,855
1951	551	1,475,560
1952	546	1,801,948
1953	541	1,842,238
1954	554	1,931,342
1955	542	2,232,297
1956	525	2,317,810

[a] Data estimated for nonreporting hospitals.
[b] Data not available.

Source: Hospitals, Aug. 1, 1957, Part 2, Vol. 31, No. 15, p. 375. Data for 1947, 1949, 1951 from Hospitals, Aug. 1955, Part 2, Vol. 29, No. 8, p. 27.

Of the $2.3 billion in total assets, $2.2 billion ($2,193,862) were plant assets. The bulk of these assets represented investment in non-Federal governmental psychiatric hospitals.

Table 3.6—Total Assets and Plant Assets in Non-Federal Psychiatric Hospitals, by Type of Ownership, 1956

Type of Ownership	Number of Hospitals	Total Assets [a]	Plant Assets [a]
		(000 omitted)	(000 omitted)
Total	525	$2,317,810	$2,193,862
Nonprofit	76	77,415	59,673
Proprietary	48	32,681	23,913
Government-non-Federal	301	2,207,714	2,110,276

[a] Data estimated for nonreporting hospitals.

Source: Hospitals, August 1, 1957, Part 2, p. 376.

As of June 30, 1956, 96 mental hospitals had been constructed with Hill-Burton Act funds. The total construction costs of these hospitals were about $86 million (National Committee Against Mental Illness, Inc., 1957, p. 14).

In 1954, the individual States spent some $86 million on "additions, improvements, and other expenditures." The data on these expenditures are presented in Table 3.7.

Arguments are often advanced to suggest that further *large* capital outlays on mental hospital facilities will not be required in the near future.[1] If this be the case, and if it is assumed that expenditures on maintenance and upkeep of existing facilities will be adequate and continuing (so that new construction is not necessary because of excessive wear and tear), then we can, at least at this level, omit the cost of construction and, in the short run, the depreciation. While we do not suggest that this practice is "orthodox," the paucity of reliable data, well defined, leaves us no other choice.[2]

Table 3.7—Expenditures (Other Than Maintenance) of
Public Prolonged-Care Hospitals, by State,
1954 [a]

State	Expenditures
United States	$89,459,430 [b]
Alabama	None
Arizona	1,703,661
Arkansas	55,530
California	9,458,339
Colorado	250,606
Connecticut	3,887,257
Delaware	270,976
District of Columbia	300,000
Florida	1,172,207
Georgia	1,231,855
Idaho	139,343
Illinois	4,415,747
Indiana	2,695,275
Iowa	1,146,984
Kansas	302,879
Kentucky	4,452,537
Louisiana	192,973
Maine	69,015
Maryland	2,471,294
Massachusetts	3,101,744 [b]
Michigan	7,810,281
Minnesota	223,327
Mississippi	201,514
Missouri	550,087
Montana	37,157
Nebraska	1,546,990
Nevada	None
New Hampshire	167,216
New Jersey	595,503
New Mexico	170,658
New York	20,849,522
North Carolina	2,210,277
North Dakota	426,918
Ohio	3,887,224
Oklahoma	102,750
Oregon	427,389
Pennsylvania	674,725
Rhode Island	38,616
South Carolina	3,348,292
South Dakota	400,655
Tennessee	241,008

State	Expenditures
Texas	1,655,413
Utah	38,437
Vermont	857,000
Virginia	931,608
Washington	797,715
West Virginia	326,486
Wisconsin	2,994,810
Wyoming	629,630

ᵃ Statistics based on reports from 214 of the 216 State and 46 of the 127 county hospitals.

ᵇ The figure for Massachusetts has been corrected and included in the total. Source showed $85,080 for Massachusetts and a total of $86,442,766 for the United States.

Source: U.S. Department of Health, Education, and Welfare, *Patients in Mental Institutions*, 1954, Part II, Table 18.

Thus, we find that, within the limits of the data and excluding capital outlays, State expenditures were in the order of about $630 million in 1955. These expenditures were for the care of those in State and county mental hospitals and State and local mental health programs. They do not include $2.25 million Federal grant-in-aid funds provided for mental health programs.

FEDERAL EXPENDITURES

In addition to the expenditures by State and local governmental units, the Federal government appropriates sums for mental health and illness purposes. These sums are of significant size.[3]

By far the largest amount is spent by the Veterans Administration. Even excluding compensation and pensions for service and nonservice connected disabilities of a mental illness nature, the Veterans Administration spends over $250 million per annum on hospital care for inpatients. An additional $5 million is spent on outpatient care. The compensation for service connected disabilities and the pensions for nonservice connected disabilities swell the total Veterans Administration expenditures by a sum slightly under $512 million. The cost of taking care of the mentally ill with Veterans Administration funds is presented in Table 3.8.

Table 3.8—Cost of Taking Care of the Mentally Ill with Veterans Administration Funds, 1956

Type	Expenditure
Total	$768,974,000
Hospital:	257,068,000
Inpatients	252,068,000
Outpatients	5,000,000
Pensions and Compensations:	
Service connected disabilities—	511,906,000
compensation:	
World War I	54,993,000
World War II	282,021,000
Spanish-American War	108,000
Regular Establishment	14,030,000
Korean	40,755,000
Nonservice connected disabilities—	
pensions:	
World War I	67,057,000
World War II	51,426,000
Spanish-American War	4,000
Korean	1,512,000

Source: Computed from Administrator of Veterans Affairs, *Annual Report, 1956.* Estimate on outpatient care furnished by National Institute of Mental Health.

Whether or not one should include compensation and pensions as part of the direct costs is arguable. One may feel that such payments should be included since they are payments that are made because mental illness is present. On the other hand, it can be argued that these payments differ substantially from expenditures on hospital care since they are, in effect, income payments, and since they may vary with the levels set by legislative action and should, therefore, be excluded.[4] We shall include these data in our direct costs (though in a separate category) because of the income aspects of these payments. We feel that it is proper to include these payments in direct costs since they are a dollar expenditure that results from the fact that there is mental illness.

In addition to the Veterans Administration expenditures, the Federal government appropriates other sums for the care of the mentally ill. These funds are spent by various agencies, including the Public Health Service, the Department of Defense, the Department of Justice, and the Department of Interior. These expenditures totaled $27 million in fiscal 1956, of which $20 million were expenditures by the Department of Defense.

Table 3.9—Expenditures by the Federal Government for the Care of the Mentally Ill, by Agency, Fiscal Year Ending June 30, 1956 [a]

Agency	Expenditure
TOTAL	$27,098,560
U.S. Public Health Service Hospital, Lexington, Kentucky	2,941,326
U.S. Public Health Service Hospital, Fort Worth, Texas	2,423,016
U.S. Public Health Service General Hospitals	456,890
Department of Defense: Inpatient Care	16,000,000
Department of Defense: Outpatient Care	4,000,000
Department of Justice, Bureau of Prisons	461,725
Department of Interior, Divisions of Territories (Alaska Morningside Hospital)	815,603

[a] Excludes those sums spent by Veterans Administration and District of Columbia expenditures included in State totals.

Source: Data supplied by National Institute of Mental Health. Letter dated July 25, 1957.

Additional Federal expenditures not related directly to the care of mental patients are also of significance. The Federal government provides $2 million in grants-in-aid to the States for mental health programs.

Table 3.10—Federal Grants-in-Aid for Mental Health, by State, 1955

	Grant-in-aid
UNITED STATES	$2,245,878
Alabama	51,034
Arizona	12,581
Arkansas	30,404
California	123,849
Colorado	19,436
Connecticut	27,018
Delaware	18,323
District of Columbia	18,149
Florida	45,361
Georgia	55,174
Idaho	18,323
Illinois	110,468
Indiana	56,209
Iowa	35,098
Kansas	27,414
Kentucky	46,576
Louisiana	42,028
Maine	17,723
Maryland	33,645
Massachusetts	63,163
Michigan	88,695
Minnesota	41,262
Mississippi	39,241
Missouri	54,749
Montana	18,323
Nebraska	16,640
Nevada	17,821
New Hampshire	18,022
New Jersey	65,845
New Mexico	18,323
New York	191,668
North Carolina	64,130
North Dakota	18,323
Ohio	109,118
Oklahoma	32,353
Oregon	19,938
Pennsylvania	141,922
Rhode Island	18,240
South Carolina	35,403
South Dakota	18,321
Tennessee	54,612
Texas	115,854

	Grant-in-aid
Utah	17,618
Vermont	18,091
Virginia	52,069
Washington	28,882
West Virginia	27,250
Wisconsin	43,233
Wyoming	7,956

Source: Interstate Clearing House on Mental Health, *Selected Tables*, 1956, Table 4.

The budget of the National Institute of Mental Health, in fiscal 1957, added another $35 million to our growing total (Budget of U.S. Government for Year ending June 30, 1958, p. 665). Much of this expenditure represents research funds. Additional Federal research funds for neuropsychiatric research of about one million dollars are allocated to the Veterans Administration (Nat. Comm. Against Mental Illness, Inc., 1957, p. 17).

Total federal expenditures, therefore, are in the order of $322 million, not including Veterans Administration payments in compensations and pensions, and in the order of $834 million including the latter. These data do not include the cost of construction of new facilities or the cost of operating mental institutions in the District of Columbia.

NONGOVERNMENTAL EXPENDITURES

We have already discussed the cost of care in State and Federal institutions. Additional nongovernmental funds are utilized both for the direct care of those mentally ill and for research and other purposes.

In 1956, the total expenses of nonprofit and proprietary mental hospitals were $78.8 million. Nonprofit mental hospitals accounted for $44 million of this total and propri-

etary hospitals for the remainder (Hospitals, 1957, p. 375).
Much of this expense is met by income derived from paying
patients. It is, nevertheless, proper to include the $79 million
as an expense associated with mental illness, while guarding
against "double counting"—i.e., not including, at a later
stage, the amount that patients pay for the services these
expenditures represent.

One of the most difficult figures to obtain with any real
confidence as to its completeness is the amount spent on
research. It has been estimated that this amount is in the
order of about $27 million. Of this, $15 million have been
included in our earlier estimate of Federal expenditures. An
additional $2 million came from private sources and $10
million from State sources (Nat. Comm. Against Mental
Illness, Inc., 1957, pp. 17-18). We shall at a later point discuss some of the reasons why it is so difficult to make reliable
estimates in this area; for the time being we shall accept the
figure indicated above.

We have thus far discussed the expenditures of the States,
of the Federal government, of proprietary and nonprofit
hospitals; and of some foundations and organizations spon-
soring research. In addition to these expenditures, individuals, themselves, finance treatment of mental illness. It
is clearly impossible to obtain complete data on this subject.
We shall, however, attempt to make some estimates of at
least part of these expenditures.

In 1955, the mean net income of psychiatrists was $17,300
per annum. Their gross income was $23,800 (Croatman,
1957b). Albee and Dickey (1957) estimated that there are
about 10,000 psychiatrists. About 40 per cent of psychiatrists
state they are in full-time private practice (Blain, 1953). If,

therefore, we assume that there are about 4000 psychiatrists in full time private practice, the public would be paying these 4000 psychiatrists, at the rate of $23,800 per year, a total of $95.2 million. Clearly, there are many additional psychiatrists in part-time private practice and the limits of the available data are such that we cannot accurately estimate the total bill that the general public is paying for private psychiatric care. It is apparent, however, that the total is large and probably in excess of $100 million per annum.

Additional sums are paid to those who are partly specializing in psychiatry and to physicians who are not in the field of psychiatry at all. It is, for example, well-known that many of the patient visits to general practitioners are related to mental problems of one sort or another. Although we would hesitate to estimate what percentage of patient visits are of this type, the percentage is considerable (The President's Commission, 1952, Vol. 2, pp. 143, 148). We have indicated that "approximately 50 per cent of patients who are treated in general practice have psychiatric complications," (see p. 4). In 1955, the mean gross income of general practitioners was almost $24,000; the net income $15,000 (Croatman, 1957a). There were approximately 86,000 general practitioners in private practice in 1955 (American Medical Association, 1956). The income of these practitioners was, therefore, in the order of $2.06 billion. Even if only 10 per cent of this income was derived from patients whose problems, directly or indirectly, were of a mental nature, the amount expended in this manner would be $206 million. If as much as 50 per cent of the income of general practitioners is derived from these sources, the total sum would be $1.03 billion per annum. This would amount to about one-third of total personal consumption expenditures for physicians' services. Although we cannot be precise in our estimates, this is clearly a sum to be reckoned with. Intensive study of general practice would, however, be required before we could accurately estimate the size of this cost component.

Table 3.11—Direct Costs of Mental Illness, by Source of Expenditure [a]

States	
Maintenance of patients in public mental hospitals (1956)	$662,146,000
Mental health (1955)	13,378,000
Research (1956)	10,000,000
Federal	
Veterans Administration, hospital care (1956), research (1957)	258,306,000
Other agencies (care of patients, 1956)	27,000,000
Grants-in-aid (1955)	2,246,000
National Institute of Mental Health (1957)	35,000,000
Foundation and other research (1956)	1,913,000
Proprietary and nonprofit voluntary hospital expenses (1956)	78,800,000
Private Psychiatry	100,000,000
Total	$1,188,789,000
Plus Veterans Administration pensions and compensation (1956)	511,906,000
Total	$1,700,695,000

[a] Does not include capital expenditures, private expenditures (nonhospital), public assistance to mentally ill, training.

The same type of estimate can be constructed for internists. We do not know what percentage of the internist's patients come to him with a mental disorder and what percentage of the internist's income comes from these patients, but we can assume that the difference between the internist and the general practitioner is, in this regard, slight. The gross income of internists in 1955 was about $23,000 (Croatman, 1957b). There were about 15,000 internists (excluding those in government service) in 1955 (American Medical Association, 1956). Their annual income was, therefore, approximately $350 million. If 10 per cent of this income was derived from patients with mental disorders, the sum paid by those patients would be $35 million; if 50 per cent was so derived, the sum would be $175 million.

In summary, then, we find that the direct costs of mental illness, as we have been able to assess these costs, are in the order of $1.7 billion.

Additional expenditures of public institutions for mental defectives and epileptics totaled $141,367,060 (not including "additions, improvements, and other expenditures") in 1954.

States spent an additional $5 million on the care of patients in psychopathic (teaching and research) hospitals in 1954.

CRITIQUE

Although we have attempted to gather as complete data as possible and have brought some of the available secondary source statistics up to date, there are many basic limitations in the original data and in their reporting. It would be a disservice to end our survey without discussing some of these limitations. This is the case for two important reasons:

1. It would be less than fair to leave the reader without a basis for evaluating the accuracy of the figures cited and without an understanding of the problems of measurement.

2. It is to be hoped that a discussion of the nature of the difficulties and of the lack, for example, of standard definitions, might lead to the correction of this situation in the future.

Although we will not present a solution to the problems and will not develop a standard reporting form (to do so would be a major undertaking requiring large expenditures

Table 3.12—Expenditures of Public Institutions for Mental Defectives and Epileptics, by State, 1954 [a]

	Maintenance Expenditures	Additions, Improvements, and Other Expenses
UNITED STATES	$141,367,060	$22,444,298
Alabama	806,707	None
Arizona	251,066	302,145
California	10,693,218	6,180,792
Colorado	1,128,564	161,089
Connecticut	4,243,271	1,489,511
Delaware	617,956	14,171
District of Columbia	892,558	212,476
Florida	896,993	296,852
Georgia	711,715	291,780
Idaho	561,855	144,754
Illinois	7,598,827	727,517
Indiana	3,998,211	566,750
Iowa	2,455,423	75,383
Kansas	2,387,837	185,355
Louisiana	833,804	98,351
Maine	1,155,863	105,302
Maryland	2,530,443	152,076
Massachusetts	10,654,459	None
Michigan	12,839,364	2,931,557
Minnesota	4,479,196	100,350
Mississippi	407,416	None
Missouri	1,542,174	103,226
Montana	459,074	237,496
Nebraska	1,075,980	15,000
New Hampshire	713,768	16,383
New Jersey	4,501,804	96,427
New Mexico	93,469	164,619
New York	27,525,249	1,537,452
North Carolina	1,593,362	486,526
North Dakota	697,242	218,025
Ohio	6,083,968	682,174
Oklahoma	1,293,617	98,474
Pennsylvania	7,930,068	344,038
Rhode Island	862,763	41,198
South Carolina	1,087,882	282,348
South Dakota	533,047	251,155
Tennessee	500,994	None
Texas	4,054,064	638,573
Utah	559,995	13,365
Vermont	423,406	11,955

	Maintenance Expenditures	Additions, Improvements, and Other Expenses
Virginia	2,103,656	1,000,791
Washington	2,926,186	98,444
West Virginia	155,707	9,419
Wisconsin	4,047,718	1,864,321
Wyoming	457,121	196,678

ª Statistics based on reports from 94 of the 97 public institutions. Arkansas and Nevada do not have public institutions for the care of mental defectives and epileptics.

Source: *Patients in Mental Institutions, 1954, Part I, Table 23.*

Table 3.13—Expenditures of Psychopathic Hospitals, by State, 1954

	Maintenance Expenditures	Additions, Improvements, and Other Expenses
UNITED STATES TOTAL	$5,239,829	$350,599
California	707,228	36,149
Colorado	575,909	271,963
Delaware	706,467	None
Indiana	1,184,691	2,843
Iowa	406,953	31,164
Massachusetts	854,091	None
Nebraska	199,298	141
New York	360,323	3,825
Tennessee	244,869	4,474

Source: *Patients In Mental Institutions, 1954, Part II, Table 19.*

of both time and funds), this section will suggest the importance of spurring efforts in this direction. In the opinion of the author, it is just as significant a contribution to explain *why,* at present, something cannot be done with complete accuracy, i.e., to explain why a question cannot be answered with precision, as it is to attempt to "come up with the right answer."

The problems of measurement are of two kinds. They

involve: (1) The completeness of the data; (2) The comparability of the data. Even before these problems arise, however, there is the more basic question, "What is it that we are trying to measure?" For the statistically inclined researcher that question, though of fundamental importance, is not one which *he* must solve. This is a question to be answered by those who present him with the problem and who will use his data.

The purposes to which the data are to be put determine the nature of the definitions to be used. For some purposes in the field of mental illness, one might want to include the costs of alcoholism, the costs of penal institutions (either in whole or in part), or other costs. For other purposes, they might be excluded. In some cases the availability of the data themselves may determine the definition used. This, however, is a situation to be deplored rather than desired. In any event, it is necessary to define the problem as specifically as possible before the measurement can begin.

Let us assume, therefore, that the definitions have been agreed upon and the data gathering embarked upon. As indicated, the difficulties that lie ahead are the result of the fact that some data are unavailable (and oftentimes cannot even be accurately estimated) and that some data, though available, cannot be added together because of lack of comparability or inadequacy of precision in definitions. In this section of our report we have faced both problems.

Exhaustiveness of Data.

We recognize that a complete accounting of the costs of mental illness and of mental health would include various items in addition to those we have discussed. Although it is hoped that we have obtained data for the major expenditure items (certainly for the major tax expenditures), a number of small and some large expenditures were unobtainable.[5] We have, for example, indicated how one might proceed to estimate the payments to psychiatrists and the payments to general practitioners and internists for services rendered in connection with mental problems. Although we think it useful to have pointed out how such data might be arrived at, in both of the above cases there were gaps in our information rendering our final figures somewhat vague. Is there anyone so rash that he would dare include such data without a good deal of knowledge about the "gaps"?

In addition, we have failed to include the expenditures on such things as drugs, lectures on mental health and illness, employer expenditures for mental health, research in basic sciences, research on university campuses (what part of a teacher's salary should be charged to research?), training programs, community resources (nonpsychiatric) for mental health, religious efforts (time devoted by clergy) toward mental health or concerned with mental illness, etc.[6] It is to be noted that most of these expenditures are of a private nature. This is, of course, not surprising, since data, in general, are harder to obtain at those levels than at governmental levels where budgets are regularly published.[7]

It is for these reasons that the margin of error in a calculation of $1.5 billion expended in tax funds is considerably less than in the $1.7 billion total direct cost figure. In both cases, however, and particularly in the grand total, the direction of error is known. The $1.7 billion is clearly an understatement of the total costs and the "true" figure may even be substantially greater.

Comparability and Consistency of Data.

In addition to the lack of various items that should be included in the total cost of mental illness, the available data have certain limitations worth noting. We shall discuss these in the same order that the original data were discussed.

In regard to State expenditures for maintenance of patients in public mental hospitals, it has been pointed out, "Great caution should be applied in making comparisons among the states on the basis of these figures, since differences in the manner of reporting and in items included or excluded tend to distort the picture and to invalidate such comparisons (Interstate Clearing House, 1956, Introduction)." The difficulty is that some States include items that other States exclude.

In an extremely interesting article, Carl E. Applegate discussed some of these problems at length. Although his chief concern was with the difficulties of using per capita cost as a means of comparison between the States, his remarks have great relevance to the question of meaningfulness of the statistical data.

Some institutions in the nation have large farms in conjunction with the hospitals and produce a major portion of the food consumed by the patients. As a part of the production of farm commodities, the question also arises as to whether or not the hospital or State charges to its operating costs the value of the farm products raised. Some States might produce certain farm commodities and not charge their value to its operating costs, or possibly only charge the cost of producing the commodity; while another State may charge to its operating cost the wholesale value of the farm product which is raised.

The method of charging and the amount of farming performed

in the hospitals throughout the nation, of course, varies greatly. In the State of California, I might say that the cost of operating the farm is charged as an operating expense but the value of the products which are raised are not included in the operating costs. In other words the cost of the farming operation is included as a part of the per capita cost. If the farms produce more than it costs them to operate then the per capita cost of the hospital is lower to that extent.

Another factor which varies throughout the nation is the amount collected as reimbursement for the care and treatment of patients. In some States the money so received will go to the general fund of the State, while in others it may be credited to the operating expenditures, thereby having the effect of reducing the per capita costs. Another factor is that of cost of construction of buildings. I believe that generally throughout the nation capital expenditures are not considered as a part of the operating costs.

There are other factors which may or may not be considered as part of the operating costs or per capita costs of a State, such as interest on investments, depreciation, cost of minor construction, heavy deferred maintenance construction works, such as bringing the physical condition of a structure up to par when no expenditures have been made for its maintenance over a period of years. Other factors which vary in methods of calculation are losses by fire and the purchase of major items of equipment. As an example, an institution may buy some new laundry machinery or new x-ray equipment. One State may charge their cost to operating expense while another may charge cost of such major equipment to a capital outlay allotment. Other factors are the cost of operating a central office of a department and whether or not such cost should be included in the overall per capita cost for the State. Then there is the cost of operating other State offices which are a service to the mental hygiene facilities of a State such as the offices of the attorney general, the state treasurer, the state controller, the personnel board, state retirement system. The retirement costs in some States might be considerable and the question arises as to whether these should be a proper charge to the operating cost of the agency or whether they should be a part of the general fund expenditures of the State. Other factors are the costs of extramural care. Does a given State charge its extramural care costs to the operations of the central office or are they charged to the per capita costs of the individual hospital? There are also the factors of cost of deportation, costs of transfer of patients among the various hospitals, as well as transportation of the patients from the county of commitment to the institution where they are received.

In addition to this some States have short-term acute treatment hospitals where the stay of the patient is relatively short. Naturally the per capita cost in such a hospital will be much higher than in another hospital caring for long-term chronic patients. The question is, "How can you compare a per capita cost between two such types of hospitals?" Likewise, there are hospitals caring for alcoholic patients which will have a different per capita cost. All of these items, to one extent or another, will affect the per capita cost, that is, the dollar per capita cost.

All of the above factors vary throughout the States of the nation and the method of computing their costs and whether or not they are charged as a part of the per capita cost of the State, of course, also varies between the individual State. These different methods of calculation, of course, nullify a true dollar per capita cost (Applegate, 1954, pp. 123–124).

We have already discussed the question of depreciation and have indicated the difficulties that arise because we have no basis for allocating the costs of capital construction. The amounts involved are considerable.

Significant sums are also involved when we consider the problem of the amounts paid by patients and their allocation. If these amounts are given to the general fund, they should not be counted again, for to do so would be to double count. If, however, they go to the State hospital and are spent by the hospital (over and above the expenditures out of the

State budget allocation), then they should be counted. We have not included these sums as a separate item and believe this decision is probably in accordance with the practices followed by most States. The amount involved is in the order of $53 million. When we deal with such sums, it is clear that intensive study of the accounting systems used would be worth while.

Table 3.14—Amounts Paid in Full or in Part for the Care of Paying Patients in Public Institutions, 1952, 1954

Institution	1954	1952
TOTAL	$52,897,000	$36,611,000
Mental defectives and epileptics	6,711,000	4,506,000
State Mental hospitals		30,241,000
County Mental hospitals	45,637,000	1,176,000
Psychopathic hospitals	549,000	688,000

Source: 1952 data, *Patients in Mental Institutions,* 1952, Part I, Table 24, Part II, Tables 37, 38, 39; 1954 data, *Patients in Mental Institutions,* 1954, Part I, Table 24, Part II, Tables 18, 19.

An additional consideration is that some of the money expended by the States for the care of the mentally ill might be expended even if the individuals involved were not mentally ill. Thus, when a person on the welfare rolls, for example, enters a mental institution, there may be no net additional cost to the State. Whether there is a financial loss or gain would depend on the previous sums expended for this individual as opposed to his costs of care in the mental institution.

We can be certain that we have not exhausted the accounting problems involved in this field. The development of standardized procedures and the testing of such procedures would certainly bring to light presently unanticipated difficulties. We have, however, mentioned the chief stumbling blocks and have pointed up the need for standardization of procedures.

At the Federal level the major difficulties probably lie in the first broad area—i.e., certain expenditures are overlooked. Yet, even in the case of the Federal government, there are some "accounting problems."

The Veterans Administration data cited earlier do not, for example, permit us to ascertain the amount spent on what we might term nonmental medical care of the mentally ill, an amount which the Veterans Administration might have to pay even if the veteran were not mentally ill. When a mentally ill veteran in a VA mental hospital has an appendectomy, we might well ask whether this cost should be charged to the costs of mental illness. The veteran, had he not been in the mental hospital, would (or might) have gone to a VA hospital for this procedure and the VA would have "paid the bill." No net additional cost, therefore, was involved. Similar problems may arise in other Federal care programs.

We would have the reader note that we are not suggesting that the costs of all nonmental health medical care be deducted from our total cost. We would deduct only the costs of those parts of the care that would have been paid for in any case under some tax-supported program. It is true, after all, that those parts which would not have come under some tax-supported program but taken care of because the individual is in a mental institution are in a sense chargeable to mental illness, it being the condition that put the State in a position where it had to bear the costs of the other conditions as well. From the point of view of the tax authorities it is mental illness that is the "villain in the piece." [8]

The same type of considerations apply to Veterans Administration pensions and compensation. In many cases the major disability is mental illness or psychoneurotic disorder. It would be useful to know what the compensation or pension level would have been for the minor disability, i.e., for the disability exclusive of mental illness.

SUMMARY

1. The direct costs of mental illness to the American economy are over $1.7 billion per annum.

2. The total obtained is an understatement of costs because it omits some items (capital construction and depreciation, some private expenditures, training, and others).

3. Additional efforts should be made to obtain more complete reporting of expenditures by groups not now reporting expenditures.

4. Further standardization of reporting procedures and more precise definitions of costs and of accounting categories would be necessary, and should be undertaken, in order that available data be made more meaningful and useful.

IV

Some Measures and Statistics of Indirect Costs

MENTAL ILLNESS, as we have shown, has a direct impact on the American economy. In financial terms, we spend money because it is present. In "real" terms, we devote resources to the fight against mental illness, resources which, if mental illness did not exist, could be devoted to the production of different goods and services.

In a larger sense, however, mental illness affects the economy because its presence reduces the total human resources available to that economy. Those individuals, for example, who are in mental institutions are not in the labor force, are not employed, do not produce goods and services. Given the full employment assumption—i.e., that, were these individuals well, they would produce goods and services—the problem before us is to measure the value of what thus is lost. The problem then is akin to that of measuring what is foregone because of unemployment. We, however, are concerned with a particular type of "unemployment," that caused by mental illness, rather than with the more general unemployment caused by instability of the economic system, e.g., the Great Depression.

In our earlier discussion, in Chapter II, we set forth the meaning of "indirect costs" and some of the philosophical problems associated with the various possible definitions and methods of measuring these costs. We now, therefore, direct our attention specifically to the statistical estimation of indirect costs, i.e., of loss in production.

It is apparent that the question, "What would those who are mentally ill contribute to society if they were not mentally ill?" is one that can only be answered by developing an estimate based on a series of assumptions. We cannot consult past records to arrive at an answer nor will we ever "know" that the answer we obtain is correct, i.e., that this would really have happened. We shall, therefore, develop a series of estimates, using various initial assumptions and data, thus approaching the problem from various directions.

ANNUAL LOSS, RESIDENT PATIENTS

We shall first be concerned with the loss to society in a given year resulting from the resident patients in State and county mental institutions. Let us be clear that this is only part, and a small part, of the total indirect costs in any given year. It does not include the loss caused by short-term absenteeism, lessened productivity while on the job, or the loss resulting from those who are mentally ill and less productive but not in the resident population in the mental hospital. Specifically, it asks, "What would those patients who are resident in public hopitals for the mentally ill have produced (earned) in a selected specific year?"

Clearly, an answer to such a question would depend on the age distribution of patients in the institutions concerned. If we assume all patients are under 15 years of age, the loss in that given year (while they are under 15) is zero (the loss in *future* earnings would, however, be greater than zero). Consider a resident population all over age 70 and the loss in the given year is also zero (the loss in future earnings would, in this case, also be zero).[1] These are trivial examples.

It is also true, however, we cannot simply say that all we would have to do to take account of age distribution would be to subtract from our total resident population those who are too young and those who are too old to work. This would be acceptable if, and only if, the same percentage of individuals in each age group were in the labor force and employed. If 100 per cent (or any other percentage) of individuals in age groups 25-34 and 55-64 were employed in the civilian labor force, we could, indeed, treat age groups 25-34 and 55-64 as one and add the number of patients in each together. This is not the case, however.

Whereas 79 per cent of the males in the age group 55-64 and 90 per cent of those 35-44 are employed, this is true of only 54 per cent of those 15-24 and of only 18 per cent 75 and over (U.S. Bureau of the Census, 1953, Table 1).

Since these differences are significant, we must know the age distribution in the hospital in order that we might know the probability (dependent on age) that the individual would be employed if he or she were not institutionalized. Furthermore, because we must know the age distribution and because age distributions change every year, our data and our results must be tied to a specific year. Our statistics will, therefore, refer only to the year 1952. They would, however, be substantially correct for any other years where the number of patients were the same and the age distribution similar.

Indeed, we could easily adjust our answer for 1952 to obtain the figure for other years, if the number of patients change, by performing a simple multiplication even without analyzing age distribution, as long as we assume the latter does not change materially in relatively short spans of time. We would simply be assuming that the age distribution of patients in 1956, for example, is the same as it was in 1952.

We shall proceed in the following manner:

1. Take State mental hospital data (male and female) and calculate the per cent of patients falling in the various age groups.

2. Assume that the patients in the "age unknown" group are distributed in the same way as those whose age is known. We cannot ignore the sizeable number in the "age unknown" group. We shall assume that they are distributed in a specified manner as are those whose age is known.

3. We shall add those individuals whose age was known and those whose age *was* unknown (but now is "known" by step 2) to obtain a total number in each age group.

4. We shall proceed as in the first three steps with the data for county hospitals.

5. We shall proceed as in the first three steps for psychopathic hospitals.

6. We shall add the results of steps 3, 4, and 5 together. We now have a total hospital population distributed by age.

7. We shall then multiply the total number in each age group by the percentage of individuals in that age group

who are employed, i.e. by the probability that these individuals, if they were not in the hospital and if they were like the rest of the population, would be employed. We shall total the various age groups. This total represents the number of individuals who would be employed out of the total number of patients in the hospital. It represents the work years lost.

8. We shall multiply the totals arrived at in step 7 by the median wage or salary income in the United States. Our product is the loss in income in the given year. Although it would be more accurate to multiply the results of step 7 by the median wage in each age group, since wages vary with age and since it cannot be assumed that the age distribution inside the hospital is the same as that found outside the hospital, recent data of the type necessary are not available.

Table 4.1—Patients Resident in State Hospitals for Mental Disease, by Age at End of Year, and Sex, 1952 [a]

| | MALE | | FEMALE | |
Age	Number	Per Cent	Number	Per Cent
Under 15	555	0.38	385	0.26
15–24	6,204	4.29	4,467	2.99
25–34	16,942	11.70	15,919	10.66
35–44	28,432	19.64	26,915	18.03
45–54	32,315	22.32	30,931	20.72
55–64	25,688	17.74	30,696	20.56
65–74	22,350	15.44	23,682	15.86
75–84	10,388	7.18	13,306	8.91
85 and over	1,902	1.31	3,003	2.01
Total	144,776	100.00	149,304	100.00

[a] Statistics based on reports from 141 of the 204 State hospitals.

Source: Patients in Mental Hospitals, 1952, Part II, Table 16.

The number of males whose age is unknown is 82,590; the number of females is 93,732. In addition, there are 37,404 patients whose age and sex is unknown. In the total hospital population, 48.3 per cent of the patients are male; 51.7 per cent are female. Allocating in those same proportions the 37,404 patients whose sex is unknown gives us 18,066 males and 19,338 females. The age-unknown males thus total 100,656 and age-unknown females total 113,070. Using the percentages found in Table 4.1, we allocate these patients as shown in Table 4.2.

Table 4.2—Age Distribution of All Patients Resident in State Hospitals for Mental Disease at End of Year, by Sex, 1952

	MALES		FEMALES	
Age	Age "Unknown"	Total	Age "Unknown"	Total
Under 15	382	937	294	679
15–24	4,318	10,522	3,380	7,847
25–34	11,777	28,719	12,053	27,972
35–44	19,769	48,201	20,387	47,302
45–54	22,466	54,781	23,428	54,359
55–64	17,856	43,544	23,247	53,943
65–74	15,541	37,891	17,933	41,615
75–84	7,227	17,615	10,075	23,381
85 and over	1,319	3,221	2,273	5,276
Total	100,655 [a]	245,431 [a]	113,070	262,374

[a] "Unknown" should add to 100,656 and total to 245,432. The differences are due to rounding error.

Source: Calculated from data in *Patients in Mental Hospitals, 1952, Part II, Table 18.*

We now proceed to carry out the same steps for county hospitals and psychopathic hospitals. The final results are shown in Tables 4.3 and 4.4.

We now total the number of patients in each age group as presented in Table 4.2, 4.3, and 4.4. These totals are multiplied by the percentage in each age group who could be expected to be employed in the civilian labor force. The product represents work years lost. These computations are presented in Table 4.5.

Table 4.3—Patients Resident in County Hospitals for Mental Disease, by Age at End of Year, and Sex, 1952

Age	MALES Age "Unknown"	Total	FEMALES Age "Unknown"	Total
Under 15	1	5	0	2
15–24	26	221	16	166
25–34	100	860	76	781
35–44	203	1,740	159	1,639
45–54	251	2,151	220	2,264
55–64	248	2,128	261	2,688
65–74	258	2,210	227	2,334
75–84	162	1,387	163	1,675
85 and over	42	359	56	577
Total	1,291 [a]	11,061 [a]	1,178 [b]	12,126 [b]

[a] "Unknown" should add to 1290 and total to 11,061. The differences are due to rounding error.

[b] "Unknown" should add to 1179 and total to 12,127. The differences are due to rounding error.

Source: Calculated from data in Patients in Mental Institutions, 1952, Part II, Table 19.

Table 4.4—Patients Resident in Psychopathic Hospitals, by Age at End of Year, and Sex, 1952

Age	MALES Age "Unknown"	Total	FEMALES Age "Unknown"	Total
Under 15	2	17	2	20
15–24	10	76	8	71
25–34	12	89	17	161
35–44	11	85	16	147
45–54	9	66	9	87
55–64	8	60	6	58
65–74	3	23	1	11
75–84	1	8	0	4
85 and over	0	0	0	3
Total	56	424	59 [a]	562 [a]

[a] "Unknown" should add to 61 and total to 564. The differences are due to rounding error.

Source: Calculated from data in Patients in Mental Institutions, 1952, Part II, Table 20.

Table 4.5—Work Years Lost by Patients in State and County Mental Hospitals and in Psychopathic Institutions, by Age, 1952

Age	MALE			FEMALE		
	Total	Per Cent Employed [a]	Work Years Lost	Total	Per Cent Employed [a]	Work Years Lost
Under 15	959	0	0	701	0	0
15–24	10,819	54	5,842	8,804	33	2,905
25–34	29,668	86	25,514	28,914	30	8,674
35–44	50,026	90	45,023	49,088	34	16,690
45–54	56,998	88	50,158	56,710	32	18,147
55–64	45,732	79	36,128	56,689	23	13,038
65–74	40,124	49	19,661	43,960	10	4,396
75 and over	22,590	18	4,066	30,916	0	927
Total	256,916		186,392	275,062		63,850

[a] Calculated from U.S. Bureau of the Census, *U.S. Census of Population: 1950*, Vol. IV, Part I, Chap. A, 1953, Table 1. Assumed Under 15 = 0.

The 1952 median wage or salary income in the United States was $3201 for males and $1398 for females (U.S. Bureau of the Census, 1954, Table 354). When we multiply these incomes by the number of work years lost (by sex), we obtain the following dollar losses.

Table 4.6—Dollar Value of Work Years Lost in 1952 by Resident Patients in Mental Institutions

Sex	Losses
TOTAL	$685,903,092
Males	596,640,792
Females	89,262,300

We thus find that, based on 1952 data, the losses total about $686 million dollars. The reader will note that we have assumed that each patient in residence in public mental hospital was there for the full year, that if he were not there he would have the same probability of employment as does any other individual, and that he would earn the average wage or salary. Clearly, these assumptions have an upward bias and we may, therefore, consider the figure of $686 million dollars as a high estimate.

Since the per cent employed varies more than the per cent in the labor force and since our previous calculations using employment data assume that an individual who is employed works for the full year (though this is taken into account when we compute the dollar values, since we assume the person earns the median annual income), it is useful to carry out the same computations as were indicated in Table 4.5 for the per cent in the total labor force.[2] Such a computation would yield data on *labor force* years lost. The results would be somewhat larger than those obtained for work years lost but would be less dependent on the particular employment situation prevailing when the data were gathered.

These data could then be adjusted to take account of the levels of employment-unemployment prevailing in any given period. The data on labor force years lost are presented in Table 4.7.

Table 4.7—Labor Force Years Lost by Patients in State and County Mental Hospitals and in Psychopathic Institutions, by Age, 1952

		MALE			FEMALE	
Age	Total	Per Cent in Labor Force [a]	Labor Force Years Lost	Total	Per Cent in Labor Force [a]	Labor Force Years Lost
Under 15	959	0	0	701	0	0
15–24	10,819	60	6,491	8,804	40	3,234
25–34	29,668	92	27,295	28,914	32	9,252
35–44	50,026	94	47,024	49,088	35	17,181
45–54	56,998	92	52,438	56,710	33	18,714
55–64	45,732	83	37,958	56,689	23	13,038
65 and over	62,714	42	26,340	74,876	10	7,488
Total	256,916		197,546	275,062		68,907

[a] From U.S. Bureau of the Census, *Statistical Abstract of the United States, 1954,* Table 217. Under 15 = 0.

When translated into dollar terms, we obtain the following losses (based, again, on a $3201 median income for males and $1398 for females).

Table 4.8—Dollar Value of Labor Force Years Lost in 1952 by Resident Patients in Mental Institutions

Sex	Losses
TOTAL	$728,676,732
Males	632,344,746
Females	96,331,986

Although it is probably true that the estimated losses obtained above are somewhat too high for the population they deal with, it is also clear that these losses are an incomplete statement of the entire problem. As has already been pointed out, it is difficult, if not impossible, to find adequate data for the noninstitutionalized population. Fortunately for our purposes, however, new and reliable data on prolonged illnesses are available. We shall use those basic data to compute the wage and salary losses resulting from mental illness. In Chapter VI we shall present information on wage and salary losses resulting from other disabilities. This will give us an opportunity to assess the significance of losses due to mental illness as compared with the losses resulting from other disorders.

LOSSES DUE TO PROLONGED
ILLNESS-ABSENTEEISM

Our basic data is survey data published by the Research Council for Economic Security. The data deal with prolonged absences from work. In the Council's survey, 176 of

the total of 6201 absences were caused by mental, psychoneurotic, and personality disorders. Mental illnesses thus accounted for 2.8 per cent of all absences (2.5 per cent of male
absences and 3.4 per cent of female absences [Research
Council, 1957, Tables 32, 33, 34]). Although accounting for
2.8 per cent of all absences, they constituted 1.6 per cent of
all absences of 5–8 weeks, 3.5 per cent of those of 9–13 weeks
duration, 4.2 per cent of those of 14–26 weeks, and 8.5 per
cent of those of more than 26 weeks (Research Council, 1957,
Table 35). Mental illness thus included a disproportionate
number of long absences. Though only 2.8 per cent of all
absences, mental disorders accounted for 4.0 per cent of all
weeks lost due to absence (3.8 per cent for males and 4.3
per cent for females [based on Research Council, 1957,
Tables 37, 38, 39]). The average duration of absences is
presented in Table 4.9.

**Table 4.9—Average Duration, in Weeks, of Prolonged
Illness-Absenteeism**

	AVERAGE DURATION	
Sex	All Illnesses	Mental
TOTAL	10.7	15.2
Male	10.8	16.7
Female	10.5	13.4

Source: Data from Research Council for Economic Security, *Prolonged Illness-
absenteeism,* 1957, Tables 37, 38, 39.

Using the above data and applying it to the American
economy in a given year, 1954, we would be able to calculate
the number of weeks lost and wages and salary income lost
as a result of that part of prolonged illness caused by mental
disability, psychoneurotic and personality disorders. We shall
proceed as follows:

1. The total number of persons employed (male and fe-

male) will be multiplied by the mental illness rate per 1000. (The sample data are weak for females as compared to males and the incidence rate is higher for females than for males. On the other hand, the sample is weak for the older age groups and the incidence rate, as shown in the sample, is lower for older than for younger individuals).

2. The product of step 1 gives us the number of individuals affected by mental illness. We then multiply the results obtained by the average weeks lost to obtain total weeks lost. This is divided by fifty to obtain work years lost.

3. Multiply work years lost by median income (wage and salary) to obtain total income lost (production foregone). The computations follow:

Table 4.10—Wages and Salaries Lost Through Mental Illness-Absenteeism, by Sex, United States, 1954

	Male	Female
(a) Total employed (1954)	42,377,000	18,861,000
(b) Mental disease rate per 1000	1	2
(c) Number affected (a) × (b)	42,377	37,722
(d) Weeks lost (average)	16.7	13.4
(e) Weeks lost (total) (c) × (d)	707,696	505,475
(f) Years lost (total) (e) ÷ 50	14,154	10,110
(g) Wage and salary income (median)	$3,201	$1,398
(h) Wage and salary loss (f) × (g)	$45,306,954	$14,133,780

Source: Data from Research Council for Economic Security, Prolonged Illness-absenteeism, 1957.

The total wage loss due to prolonged absence is $59,440,734. This is, of course, a very rough estimate, since we have projected the same rates found in private nonagricultural employment to the total economy. Nevertheless, it affords some guide to the order of magnitude of the losses from that part of mental illness that is short term (the bulk of the individuals returned to their jobs). How many of the individuals in this analysis were also included in our computations for the resident hospital population is unknown. Because of the—for mental illness—short duration of the disability, it is probable that relatively few were hospitalized in public institutions and, therefore, little if any "double counting" is involved if we add this $60 million to our earlier total.[3]

FUTURE LOSSES, FIRST ADMISSIONS

Although it is possible, as we have shown, to examine the losses in any particular year attributable to mental illness, using as a base the resident patients in mental hospitals, it is also useful to examine the losses which will be incurred over a period of time, using first admissions to mental hospitals as a base. In adopting this approach, we are saying, "Here is a group that is admitted to the mental hospital for the first time. This group of males and females has a particular age distribution. If the individual were not in this group, we would assume that his life expectancy and work-years expectancy would be the same as that of the same age group in the total population. What is this working-years expectancy, i.e., how many years would similar age individuals expect to work? What, then, do we lose as a result of the admission of this individual and what do we lose as a result of the admission of the entire group?" To answer this question, we shall need various data not relating to mental illness (in order to compute expected working years) and specific data relating to mental illness and first admissions. We shall first compute "expected working years" by age group, male and female. The results will be utilized for various purposes in our later analysis and are, therefore, presented in some detail.[4]

Table 4.11—Expected Labor Force Years, Males, United States

(1 Age	(2) Per Cent in Labor Force	(3) Number Attaining Age X [a]	(4) Average Number in Labor Force of 1000 Live Births [b]	(5) Total Future Labor Force Years [c]	(6) Expected Labor Force Years [d]
Under 14		937		36,767	39
14 and 15	15.5	935	145	36,622	39
16–17	35.9	932	335	36,142	39
18–19	66.8	929	621	35,186	38
20–24	81.9	922	755	32,678	35
25–34	92.1	905	834	26,620	29
35–44	94.5	873	825	18,325	21
45–54	92.0	808	743	10,485	13
55–64	83.4	680	567	3,935	6
65 and over	41.5	529 [e]	220	550	1

[a] Of 1000 live births.

[b] Column 2 times Column 3.

[c] Computed by: The sum of (the number of years in the age group times the average number in labor force of 1000 live births, i.e., Column 4, for all succeeding age groups plus one-half of the years in the age group concerned times the figure in Column 4 associated with that age group). Thus: $36,767 = (2)(145) + 2(335) + 2(621) + 5(755) + 10(834) + 10(825) + 10(743) + 10(567) + 5(220) + (7)(0)$; $36,622 = 2(335) + 2(621) + 000 + 5(220) + 1(145)$; etc. We use 5 years for the age group 65 and over in accordance with note e.

[d] Column 5 divided by Column 3.

[e] Assume all individuals 65 and over cease working by age 70. Life expectancy figure is for age 67.5.

Source: Column 2 from U.S. Bureau of the Census, *U.S. Census of Population, 1950*, Table 1; Column 3 from Dublin and Lotka, *The Money Value of A Man*, 1946, Table 47.

The last columns, "expected labor force years," in Tables 4.11 and 4.12 are significant for our purposes. With unemployment at low levels, expected labor force years are virtually equivalent to expected working years. Thus we have computed the average working years that the males and females in various age groups can look forward to (having taken into account the fact that some individuals do not enter the labor force and that some die). Table 4.11, for example, indicates that, on the average, a male age 25-34 can expect to have 29 years of working life left. Thus, if 100 individuals aged 25-34 were to be killed, society would lose (100) (29) = 2900 working (labor force) years. If we assume that an individual who enters a mental institution never works again, and if we know his or her age at entry, it is easy (using Tables 4.11 and 4.12) to see the number of working years lost because of mental illness.

Table 4.12—Expected Labor Force Years, Females, United States

(1)	(2)	(3)	(4)	(5)	(6)
Age	Per Cent in Labor Force	Number Attaining Age X [a]	Average Number in Labor Force of 1000 Live Births	Total Future Labor Force Years	Expected Labor Force Years
Under 14	——	950	——	14,242	15
14 and 15	5.1	949	48	14,194	15
16 and 17	17.8	947	169	13,977	15
18 and 19	43.8	945	414	13,394	14
20–24	43.2	940	406	11,965	13
25–34	31.8	927	295	9,475	10
35–44	35.0	901	315	6,425	7
45–54	32.9	855	281	3,445	4
55–64	23.4	764	179	1,145	1
65 and over	7.8	640	50	125	0

[a] Of 1000 live births.

Source: Column 2 from U.S. Bureau of the Census, U.S. Census of Population, 1950, Table 1; Column 3 from Dublin and Lotka, The Money Value of A Man, 1946, Table 50.

It is now possible to calculate the dollar loss of earning power over the individual's lifetime. We shall, for the moment, assume that an individual who enters a mental institution will not work again. Clearly, this is an assumption that is in error. It will, however, give us the largest possible figure. What we would really like to know for every age group of first admissions is the length of stay in the hospital, time of discharge, time of return to hospital (if there is a return), time of discharge, and so on. It is not sufficient to know only the average duration of stay over a lifetime by age group (though this would be helpful), since we need to know not only how much an individual can be expected to earn if he is discharged but also *when* he will earn this wage or salary, when he will return to the hospital, when he will again start working, etc. Such data are unavailable. We shall, therefore, first assume that those who enter the hospital never leave it. This is the simplest assumption and yields the largest total loss. Subsequently we shall relax this assumption.

In order to carry out our calcuations, we shall discount future earnings to the present. It is obvious that $1000 twenty years from now is worth less than $1000 today. How much it is worth today depends on the rate of interest. With a 2 per-cent rate of interest, $672.97 today will be worth $1000 in twenty years; at a 3 per-cent rate, today's sum need only be $553.68; at 4 per cent, $456.39. The present value of a sum due at the end of n years depends both on n and on r, the rate of interest and is given by the expression $\dfrac{1}{(1 + r)^n}$

It is necessary to discount future earnings to the present in order to have a more meaningful total and in order to be better able to assess the real economic loss involved. Although humanitarian considerations may be sufficient to suggest that expenditures on research to combat mental illness are worth while, discounting future earnings to the present would help make possible an assessment of the economic value of such research expenditures.

In economic terms, given a rate of interest of 4 per cent, it would not "pay" to spend $800 today in order to have an additional $1000 twenty years hence. It would, however, "pay" if one could spend $456.39 or less. In order to provide means to assess the economic value of expenditures, we shall discount future earnings to the present. This is akin to what the businessman would do to assess whether or not a particular investment, undertaken and paid for today, will be profitable. The present values of discounted future earnings for males are presented in Tables 4.13 and 4.14.

Table 4.13—Present Value of Future Expected Income Based on 4% Rate of Interest, Males

Age	Expected Work Years	Expected Income (at $3201 Per Annum)	One-half Expected Life [a] = n	Discounting Factor (1.04) [n]	Present Value at 4%
Under 15	39	$124,839	27	2.8834	$43,296
15–24	37	118,437	25	2.6658	44,428
25–34	29	92,829	19	2.1068	44,062
35–44	21	67,221	15	1.8009	37,326
45–54	13	41,613	11	1.5395	27,030
55–64	6	19,206	7	1.3159	14,595
65 and over	1	3,201	5	1.2167	2,631

[a] It is assumed that all of the loss comes at the midpoint of the remainder of the life expectancy. Data from Dublin and Lotka, *The Money Value of A Man,* 1946, Table 47.

Since rates of interest change, we have also calculated the present value of future expected earnings at rates other than the 4 per cent assumed in Table 4.13. We shall carry out our calculations assuming a 4 per cent rate. The reader can refer to Table 4.14 if he prefers some other rate.

Table 4.14—Present Value of Future Expected Income at Various Rates of Interest, Males

Age	2%	2.5%	3%	3.5%	4.5%	5%
Under 15	$73,138	$64,092	$56,201	$49,313	$38,037	$33,438
15–24	72,191	63,884	56,567	50,117	39,408	34,974
25–34	63,721	58,067	52,939	48,286	40,223	36,735
35–44	49,946	46,414	43,146	40,124	34,734	32,335
45–54	33,468	31,715	30,062	28,503	25,642	24,330
55–64	16,720	16,157	15,616	15,096	14,113	13,649
65 and over	2,899	2,829	2,761	2,695	2,569	2,508

We are now ready to compute the losses to society, discounted to the present, of the male first admissions to public prolonged-care hospitals for mental disease in 1954. In that year, 54,716 males whose age distribution was known and 11,545 whose ages were unknown were admitted. We shall adjust for the age-unknown group as a final step. We assume a rate of interest of 4 per cent (a lower rate of interest would yield a higher total loss).

Table 4.15—Present Value of Future Earnings of First Admissions to Public Prolonged-Care Hospitals for Mental Disease, by Age, Male, 1954

Age	Number of First Admissions [a]	Present Value of Individual Future Earnings	Total Present Value of Future Earnings
Under 15	754	$43,296	$ 32,645,184
15–24	5,616	44,428	249,507,648
25–34	9,690	44,062	426,960,780
35–44	10,552	37,326	393,863,952
45–54	8,826	27,030	238,566,780
55–64	6,234	14,595	90,985,230
65 and over	3,223 [b]	2,631	8,479,713
Total	44,895		$1,441,009,287

[a] Patients in Mental Institutions, 1954, Part II, Table 7.
[b] Omits age 75 and over and takes one-half of the 65 to 75 group (retirement at age 70 is assumed).

If the age-unknown group, 11,545 in number, were distributed by age in the same proportions as was the age-known group, the total shown in Table 4.15 would be swelled by 21 per cent (after adjustment of 11,545 by the proportion age 70 and over). This would raise the total arrived at in Table 4.14 to $1,743,621,237. The present (1954) value of all expected future earnings (discounted at 4 per cent) of males who entered public prolonged-care hospitals in 1954 was thus over $1.7 billion.

Table 4.16—Per Cent of First Admissions to New York Civil State Hospitals Discharged and Dying During Specified Periods After Admissions, Males [a]

| | DISCHARGED (per cent) | | | | | | DEATHS (per cent) | | | | | |
	1st Year	2nd Year	3rd Year	4th Year	5th Year	Total	1st Year	2nd Year	3rd Year	4th Year	5th Year	Total
Under 15	33.3	16.0	9.9	4.8	3.3	67.3	1.0	0.2	0.6	0.4	——	2.2
15–19	27.0	37.3	8.9	2.9	1.2	77.3	1.2	0.4	0.4	0.4	0.4	2.8
20–24	27.2	34.1	6.9	3.5	1.7	73.4	1.8	0.6	0.3	——	0.3	3.0
25–29	26.9	34.7	6.2	2.2	1.3	71.3	2.6	0.7	0.4	0.2	0.6	4.5
30–34	24.3	36.2	6.7	3.1	1.6	71.9	3.4	0.4	0.5	1.1	0.6	6.0
35–39	22.3	34.3	5.9	2.4	1.1	66.0	7.4	1.6	1.2	0.4	0.5	11.1
40–44	20.3	34.0	5.3	2.1	1.2	62.9	9.2	2.2	1.6	0.2	0.4	13.6
45–49	17.9	30.9	5.8	1.9	0.8	57.3	13.7	3.0	1.0	0.8	——	18.5
50–54	14.2	26.9	4.5	0.9	0.5	47.0	18.9	3.6	3.8	1.4	1.5	29.2
55–59	11.8	23.8	3.9	1.6	0.2	41.3	25.4	4.1	2.6	1.9	1.8	35.8
60–64	7.8	16.3	2.1	1.4	0.2	27.8	34.2	7.2	4.7	3.5	1.8	51.4
65–69	5.6	11.8	1.9	1.2	——	20.5	42.7	8.7	5.7	3.6	3.4	64.1
70 and over	3.3	4.0	0.4	0.3	0.1	8.1	61.7	9.1	5.5	3.8	2.8	82.9

[a] Classified according to age at first admission.

Source: Malzberg, 1956, "Cohort Studies of Mental Disease," Mental Hygiene, Vol. 40, Tables 5, 11.

As was previously pointed out, the total figure arrived at for the loss of earnings was undoubtedly too large for the population it dealt with, since it assumed that individuals who enter the mental institution never work again. National data of the type we would need on admissions, discharges, and readmissions in order to examine the length of stay in hospitals are not available, but there do exist certain bodies of data which may be adapted for our purposes. We now turn to these data in order to make the adjustments necessary.

In a recent article, Benjamin Malzberg (1956) examined the experience of 64,573 patients representing the first admissions to the New York Civil State hospitals in the period 1943–1949. He provides us with reliable data for this population. We shall utilize these data and apply them to the national scene. In particular, we shall use the data on deaths and discharge by age group in the first five years after admission. These data for males are presented in Table 4.16.

When we combine the data in Table 4.16 with our earlier data on expected working years by age, we arrive at a better approximation to the total years lost than we were able to obtain by assuming that those who enter the mental hospitals never leave. Our approach can be summarized as follows:

1. Assume 1000 first admissions in each age group.

2. We lose all remaining working years for those who die in the first five years.

3. We lose all remaining working years for those still in the hospital after five years. (This overstates the case somewhat, but probably not appreciably, since the probability of discharge except through death for those still in the institution after five years is low.)

4. We lose one year for those discharged in the first year, two years for those discharged in the second year, and so forth. (This assumes that, once discharged, a patient does not enter the hospital again. This downward bias is partially balanced by the fact that we assume a patient loses an entire year when, in fact, it may be a fraction of a year.)

5. We add the results of steps 3, 4, and 5. The total represents total working years lost. When divided by total expected working years we have the fraction of total working years lost.

We thus find that of every 1000 males between 20–24 representing 35,000 future expected working years we lose: 1050 years for the 30 who die; 8260 years for the 236 still in the hospital after 5 years; 272 for the 272 who only stay a year or less; 682 for the 341 patients discharged in their second year; 207 years for the 69 who are discharged in their third year; 140 for the 35 patients discharged in their fourth year, and 85 for the 17 patients discharged in their fifth year. Similar computations can be made for each age group. These are presented in Table 4.17.

Table 4.17—Expected Working Years Lost by Death and Residence in Hospital, 1000 First Admissions in Each Age Group, Males

LOSS IN YEARS

Age	Through Death	In Hospital After Five Years	Stay in Hospital Up To Five Years	Total	Total Expected Working Years	Per Cent of Expected Work Years Lost
Under 15	858	11,895	——[a]	12,753	39,000	33
15–19	1,064	7,562	1,459	10,085	38,000	27
20–24	1,050	8,260	1,386	10,696	35,000	31
25–29	1,395	7,502	1,302	10,199	31,000	33
30–34	1,620	5,697	1,372	8,959	27,000	33
35–39	2,553	5,267	1,237	9,057	23,000	39
40–44	2,584	44,465	1,186	8,235	19,000	43
45–49	2,775	3,630	1,087	7,492	15,000	50
50–54	3,212	2,618	876	6,706	11,000	61
55–59	2,864	1,832	785	5,481	8,000	69
60–64	2,056	832	531	3,419	4,000	86
65–69	641	154	205	1,000	1,000	100

[a] We assume no work years lost while in hospital since this group is under 15.

The results of our analysis are summarized in Table 4.18.

Table 4.18—Expected Working Years Lost Through Death
and Failure to be Discharged Within Five
Years; Years Lost Through All Causes, 1000
First Admissions in Each Age Group, Males

Age	Total Years Lost Through Death and Remaining in Hospital After Five Years	Per Cent of Expected Work Years Lost	Total Years Lost Including Years till Discharge [a]	Per Cent of Expected Work Years Lost [b]
Under 15	12,753	33	12,753	33
15–19	8,626	23	10,085	27
20–24	9,310	27	10,696	31
25–29	8,897	29	10,199	33
30–34	7,587	28	8,959	33
35–39	7,820	34	9,057	39
40–44	7,049	37	8,235	43
45–49	6,405	43	7,492	50
50–54	5,830	53	6,706	61
55–59	5,481	59	5,481	69
60–64	2,888	72	3,419	86
65–69	795	80	1,000	100
Total	83,441	33	94,082	38

[a] See Column 5, Table 4.17.
[b] See Column 7, Table 4.17.

We now have statistics which are of value because of their general nature. The reader will note that these were calculated using 1000 admissions in each age group as a base. Although the same *percentage* would be lost in each age group no matter what the absolute number of admissions, the *total* percentage would be different with unequal size age groups (i.e., unequal number of first admissions). One could easily adjust for this difference if one desired to assess the years lost by first admissions in any State or in the nation. Thus, the basic results remain useful even as patterns of patient admission change. The method of adjusting the data is presented in Table 4.19. In this computation, we shall use

as our base the 1954 data on first admissions to public prolonged-care hospitals for mental disease.

**Table 4.19—Expected Working Years Lost, First Admis-
sions to Public Prolonged-Care Hospitals for
Mental Disease, by Age, 1954, Males**

(1)	(2)	(3)	(4)	(5)	(6)
		Years Lost Per 1000	Actual	Per Cent	Per Cent
Age	Admissions [a]	Admissions [b]	Loss [c] Years	of Loss	by Admissions
Under 15	754	12,753	9,616	2.8	1.7
15–24	5,616	10,390	58,350	16.9	12.5
25–34	9,690	9,579	92,821	26.8	21.6
35–44	10,552	8,646	91,224	26.4	23.5
45–54	8,826	7,099	62,656	18.1	19.7
55–64	6,234	4,450	27,741	8.0	13.9
65–74	3,223 [d]	1,000	3,223	0.9	7.2
Total	44,895	——	345,631	99.9	100.1

[a] *Patients in Mental Institutions, 1954, Part II, Table 7.*
[b] Table 4.18 age groups consolidated.
[c] Column 3 times column 2 divided by 1000.
[d] One-half of 6446.

Using our earlier assumption that once a patient is admitted
to the mental institution he never re-enters the labor force,
we would find (after adding 21 per cent to take account of
the age-unknown category), a loss in male labor-force years
totaling 1,083,150. The discounted dollar value represented
by these years was $1.7 billion. We indicated that those data
were an overstatement of the problem because patients do
return to work from the hospital.

Our revised data using the Malzberg discharge and death
rates run much lower. This is because we now allow the
patient to be discharged (although not readmitted), and
because we assume that when discharged he is re-employed.
The adjusted male work-years lost total 418,214, and the
dollar loss, though it cannot be estimated accurately without

discounting computations, totals around .7 billion. The adjusted data understate the real loss, however, since they assume no readmissions and further assume that the individual finds employment when discharged. The true answer, then, lies somewhere between these extremes of $.7 and $1.7 billion.[5] Further statistical study of employment rates and readmission patterns for discharged patients would be required before we could state which of these approximations is more accurate.

We have illustrated our technique in considerable detail in order that the reader might be better able to follow the argument and in order that he might see how the results can be applied to any population one cares to study. Having developed the technique once, it is not necessary to present all the computations again in the discussion of losses in *female* first admissions. It will, therefore, suffice to present only final results and tables.

We have already shown (Table 4.12) the expected working life for females. If we use the results presented in Table 4.12 to calculate the present value of future expected income (using an average income of $1398) as was done for males (Tables 4.13, 4.14), we obtain the discounted values shown in Table 4.20.

We shall, as was done for males in Table 4.15, select a 4 per cent rate of interest for discounting purposes. In reviewing our results the reader should note that we have ignored the economic value of the housewife and have addressed ourselves solely to the loss in earning power of women in the labor force. Had we included the housewife's services as work years, and the housewife as an individual participating in the labor force, the expected working years for females

Table 4.20—Present Value of Future Expected Income at Various Rates of Interest, Female

Age	2%	2.5%	3%	3.5%
Under 15	$11,577	$10,247	$8,899	$7,733
15–24	11,696	10,299	9,075	8,002
25–34	9,224	8,324	7,515	6,788
35–44	6,989	6,431	5,921	5,453
45–54	4,409	4,158	3,922	3,701
55–64	1,193	1,147	1,104	1,062

Age	4%	4.5%	5%
Under 15	6,724	5,851	5,095
15–24	7,059	6,232	5,504
25–34	6,135	5,547	5,018
35–44	5,024	4,631	4,270
45–54	3,493	3,297	3,114
55–64	1,022	983	946

would be increased appreciably. Were we to then impute to the housewife the median wage or salary income enjoyed by working women, the expected future earnings of females would increase substantially (as would the money losses resulting from an admission into the hospital). The reader is

Table 4.21—Present Value of Future Earnings of First Admissions to Public Prolonged-Care Hospitals for Mental Disease, by Age, Female, 1954

Age [a]	Number of First Admissions [b]	Present Value of Individual Future Earnings	Total Present Value of Future Earnings
Under 15	427	$6,724	$ 2,871,148
15–24	3,930	7,059	27,741,870
25–34	8,037	6,135	49,306,995
35–44	7,679	5,024	38,579,296
45–54	5,999	3,493	20,954,507
55–64	4,410	1,022	4,507,020
Total	30,482		$143,960,836

[a] Omit 65 and over since expected working years and income are zero.
[b] *Patients in Mental Institutions, 1954, Part II, Table 7.*

referred to the discussion in Chapter II for clarification of the reasons for the omission.

We must raise the total obtained to take account of the 11,000 females whose age is unknown. We shall assume that these 11,000 have the same age distribution as the females whose age is known. This would, therefore, raise our total by 27 per cent (after adjustment for those aged 65 and over) and bring it to $182,830,261. Our total is, of course, substantially below the equivalent figure for males ($700 million). There are four reasons for the differences:

1. Fewer female first admissions than male (only about 67 per cent in the relevant age groups).

2. Lower median income for females than for males.

3. Less labor force participation on the part of females, therefore, fewer expected working years (and total earnings).

4. Greater life expectancy for females, therefore a greater discounting factor.

It is interesting, at this point to compare the losses with the passage of time (i.e., in total future earnings) to the losses incurred in the first year of admission. The reader will recall that earlier we had computed the losses in a given year for all resident patients. We now do the same for the first admissions. We use the same labor force participation rates originally presented in Table 4.7 and multiply first admissions in each age group by these labor force participation rates in order to obtain the labor force years lost in the first year after the first admission. The total male labor force years lost equals 36,824; for females the total is 9,826. When multiplied by median wage and salary income, the loss equals $117,873,624 for males and $13,736,748 for females. To take account of the first admissions whose age is unknown, we must raise the male total by 21 per cent and the female total by 27 per cent (in a manner similar to the preceding analysis on total future earnings). Our losses then are $142,627,085 for males and $16,621,465 for females. The relationship between the losses in the first year and all discounted future losses is shown in Table 4.22.

Table 4.22—Income Lost in First Year and Through Time (Discounted at 4 Per Cent) for First Admissions to Public Prolonged-Care Hospitals for Mental Disease

	Losses in First Year	All Future Losses (Discount at 4%)	Per Cent Lost in First Year
Total	$159,248,550	$1,926,451,498	8.3
Male	142,627,085	1,743,621,237	8.2
Female	16,621,465	182,830,261	9.1

The reader must be reminded, however, that it would be incorrect to say that the losses in the first year run about 8 per cent of total losses as time passes. He should note that the total losses assume an individual will not work again and are, therefore, an overstatement of the dollar losses. The losses incurred in the first year of admission are, on the other hand, much closer to the correct figure, since only a relatively small proportion of patients are discharged during the first year (though many die) and most of these probably lose the full year's work. It is, therefore, significant to note that $160 million are lost (1954 data) in the first year following the first admission.[6] If we compare the first years' losses to adjusted future losses (using Malzberg data and assuming that patients *are* discharged) the $160 million are to be compared to $.8 billion (.7 for males and .1 for females [female computations follow our present discussion]). This ratio equals 20 per cent.

It is now possible to relax the assumption that females who enter the mental hospital will never work again. We shall follow the same approach used in analyzing the male population and shall again utilize the basic data gathered by Malzberg (1956). The results of our calculations are presented in Table 4.23. This table is comparable to Table 4.18 for males.

Table 4.23—Expected Working Years Lost Through Death and Failure to be Discharged Within Five Years; Years Lost Through All Causes, 1000 First Admissions in Each Age Group, Females

	Total Years Lost Through Death and Remaining in Hospital After Five Years	Per Cent of Expected Work Years Lost	Total Years Lost Including Years till Discharge	Per Cent of Expected Work Years Lost
Under 15	4,560	30	6,314	42
15–19	3,540	24	5,083	34
20–24	3,237	25	4,683	36
25–29	3,245	30	4,595	42
30–34	2,610	29	4,010	45
35–39	2,600	33	3,940	49
40–44	2,172	36	3,432	57
45–49	2,100	42	3,290	66
50–54	1,362	45	2,420	81
55–59	1,106	55	1,913	96
60–64	688	69	1,000	100

The differences between males and females are due to the fact that the rates of discharge (and time of discharge) and death differ and also to the fact that women have a lower labor force years expectancy figure (the latter means that when a woman is in the hospital for, say, two years she loses a greater percentage of her working years than does a male).

We are now in a position to assess the losses resulting from the 1954 female first admissions to public prolonged-care hospitals for mental disease.

Table 4.24—Expected Working Years Lost, First Admissions to Public Prolonged-Care Hospitals for Mental Disease, by Age, 1954, Females

Age	Admissions [a]	Years Lost Per 1000 Admissions [a]	Actual Loss (Years)	Per Cent of Loss	Per Cent by Admissions
Under 15	427	6,314	2,696	2.5	1.4
15–24	3,930	4,883	19,190	17.7	12.9
25–34	8,037	4,302	34,575	31.9	26.4
35–44	7,679	3,686	28,305	26.1	25.2
45–54	5,999	2,875	17,247	15.9	19.7
55–64	4,410	1,456	6,421	5.9	14.5
Total	30,482		108,434	100.0	100.1

[a] Patients in Mental Institutions, 1954, Part II, Table 7.

As before, we should raise the total arrived at by 27 per cent to take account of the 11,000 females whose age is unknown. We then have a total labor force years lost equal to 137,711 years.

Using our earlier assumption that a patient never re-enters the labor force once she has been admitted to the hospital, we would find a loss (after adding 27 per cent to take account of the age unknown category) of 284,422 labor force years. The present value of all future earnings in those years was $183 million. The true figure must be between these figures and the adjusted data (based on Malzberg) which permit the patient to be discharged. These result in a loss of 137,711 years (and a dollar loss somewhere near 90 million).

We shall reserve for a later discussion (Chapter VI) the analysis of working years lost by diagnostic category. These data are significant since they point up the fact that the number of working years lost is a function of two variables: the number of admissions in each diagnostic category and the age of admission. Our analysis of the manner in which both factors affect the total working years lost will shed light on the significance (in terms of indirect costs) of the various diagnostic categories of mental illness. We reserve this discussion for a later time, however, in order to limit our considerations at this time to the *total* figures.

SUMMARY

1. This chapter illustrates the techniques that can be utilized in attempting to calculate indirect costs of mental illness.

2. It utilizes available data, gathered for other purposes, and shows how to rearrange these data to provide types of information necessary for cost analysis.

3. It provides basic data on losses in labor force years. These data can be applied in the various States to show how resident patients in, and first admissions to, State hospitals impinge on the individual State's economy.

4. By the use of the techniques indicated we arrive at the following cost estimates:

a) Losses in 1952, for all patients resident in mental institutions, were $700 million in that one year.

b) Present value of all future earnings of first admissions to public prolonged-care hospitals (1954) was $1.9 billion.

c) Losses during the first year for first admissions (1954) were $160 million.

d) Based on probable discharge and death rates (but not including readmissions), first admissions (1954) will lose 556,000 labor force years in their remaining years of life. This is equal to a present value of about $800 million.

e) Age group 25–34 accounted for the greatest indirect loss (over time) to the economy.

5. The losses indicated apply only to the population discussed and do not include private patients, veterans, and other groups and do not attempt to measure the loss due to lower productivity on the part of those who stay at work. Nor do they include the value of housewives' services. The same, or similar, techniques could be applied to those groups. Actual losses in the economy would, therefore, be higher than our data indicate.

V

Significance of Direct Costs

WE HAVE previously (Chapter III) presented statistical information relating to direct costs and have discussed some of the shortcomings of the available data. It was because of the problems of completeness and comparability that we stated that the estimate of total direct costs of $1.7 billion were only an approximation to the actual expenditures on mental illness and health and that the true figures might run many millions more. In spite of the limitations of the data, it is possible, nevertheless, to assess the importance and the meaning of this expenditure by examining it (or parts of it) in relation to various other expenditures and by measuring the savings resulting from discharge of patients from the mental hospital. We shall use these different approaches in our discussion of the significance of the direct expenditures on mental illness.

DIRECT COSTS AS A FUNCTION OF TIME

One of the important, and interesting, questions that might be asked of the individual doing research in this area would be, "What will be the total cost, as time passes, of taking care of the patient who enters the mental hospital?" Clearly, no answer can be given to this question unless more information is provided on such matters as sex, age, and mental disorder of the particular individual.

We have, however, already indicated our belief that the question is both interesting and important and it therefore behooves us to attempt to answer it. Although no answer is possible for the individual patient, we can, however, adopt the statistician's device of talking about a group of patients. We do not know very much about one individual and thus cannot predict in such a case, but we do, in a statistical sense, know much about the group—and can predict for it. We would, furthermore, argue that we will answer the question in terms of a group not only because that is the only way the question can be answered but because that really is the more interesting question—i.e., that is the way the question should have been asked. From the standpoint of society, we are not really concerned, after all, with what this particular patient who enters the hospital will cost the State in a given period of time, but rather with what this *group* of patients will cost (from which, of course, an average per patient may be derived although it may be the case that the "average" patient does not even exist).

We shall, for our analysis, assume a hypothetical population of 10,000 first admission patients. These patients have a particular age and sex distribution. We can, of course, assume any age and sex distribution we desire, but the more realistic the age and sex characteristics we select, the more general usefulness our answers will have. Furthermore, we will have to apply death and discharge data to this population and such data are more applicable if we select a population with "real world" characteristics.

Our population will, therefore, be distributed as was the population entering New York State Mental institutions in the period 1943–1949 (Malzberg, 1956). We take our group of 10,000 patients and classify them by age and sex in similar proportions to the population Malzberg examined. The New York data included 30,226 males whose ages were known (46.91 per cent) and 34,207 females (53.09 per cent) of known ages; our hypothetical 10,000 will therefore include 4691 males and 5309 females. Our population will, therefore, be distributed as indicated in Table 5.1.

Table 5.1—Hypothetical 10,000 First Admissions, by Age and Sex [a]

Age	Male	Female
Under 15	92	35
15–19	209	188
20–24	278	315
25–29	277	373
30–34	294	405
35–39	309	402
40–44	323	366
45–49	311	360
50–54	323	366
55–59	348	325
60–64	368	321
65–69	372	369
70 and over	1,187	1,484
Total	4,691	5,309

[a] Distributed as New York State 1943–1949 first admissions (Malzberg, 1956, Table 3). The figure of 9,670 for females 70 or over in the original Malzberg data is obviously an error and should be 9,560.

We shall assume that our hypothetical population has the same proportion of deaths and discharges as did the population under consideration. This assumption is the same one that we made earlier (Chapter IV) when we considered

Table 5.2—Years of Patient Care, Hypothetical First Admissions, Discharge and Death Rates as Per New York State 1943–1949, Males and Females [a]

Age	Number Admissions	1st Year Deaths	1st Year Discharges	1st Year Total	1st Year .5 Total	Years of Patient Care 1st Year	Number Starting 2nd Year	2nd Year Deaths	2nd Year Discharges	Years of Patient Care in 2nd Year
MALE										
Under 15	92	1	31	32	16	76	60	0	15	52.5
15–19	209	3	56	59	29.5	179.5	150	1	78	110.5
20–24	278	5	76	81	40.5	237.5	197	2	95	148.5
25–29	277	7	75	82	41	236	195	2	96	146
30–34	294	10	71	81	40.5	253.5	213	1	106	159.5
35–39	309	23	69	92	46	263	217	5	106	161.5
40–44	323	30	66	96	48	275	227	7	110	168.5
45–49	311	43	56	99	49.5	261.5	212	9	96	159.5
50–54	323	61	46	107	53.5	269.5	216	12	87	166.5
55–59	348	88	41	129	64.5	283.5	219	14	83	170.5
60–64	368	126	29	155	77.5	290.5	213	26	60	170
65–69	372	159	21	180	90	282	192	32	44	154
70 and over	1,187	732	39	771	385.5	801.5	416	108	47	338.5
Total	4,691	1,288	676	1,964	982	3,709	2,727	219	1,023	2,106
FEMALE										
Under 15	35	1	6	7	3.5	31.5	28	0	7	24.5
15–19	188	2	37	39	19.5	168.5	149	1	80	108.5
20–24	315	7	63	70	35	280	245	3	143	172
25–29	373	7	72	79	39.5	333.5	294	2	154	216
30–34	405	13	71	84	42	363	321	4	174	232
35–39	402	18	63	81	40.5	361.5	321	6	168	234
40–44	366	24	50	74	37	329	292	6	153	212.5
45–49	360	37	41	78	39	321	282	11	133	210
50–54	366	51	41	92	46	320	274	11	130	203.5
55–59	325	69	28	97	48.5	276.5	228	16	92	174
60–64	321	100	22	122	61	260	199	18	64	158
65–69	369	143	20	163	81.5	287.5	206	32	49	165.5
70 and over	1,484	825	45	870	435	1,049	614	168	62	499
Total										2,609.5

Age	3rd Year	Deaths	Discharged	in 3rd Year	4th Year	Deaths	Discharged	Parent Care in 4th Year
				MALE				
Under 15	45	1	9	40	35	0	4	33
15–19	71	1	19	61	51	1	6	47.5
20–24	100	1	19	90	80	0	10	75
25–29	97	1	17	88	79	1	6	75.5
30–34	106	1	20	95.5	85	3	9	79
35–39	106	4	18	95	84	1	7	80
40–44	110	5	17	99	88	1	7	84
45–49	107	3	18	96.5	86	2	6	82
50–54	117	12	15	103.5	90	5	3	86
55–59	122	9	14	110.5	99	7	6	92.5
60–64	127	17	8	114.5	102	13	5	93
65–69	116	21	7	102	88	13	4	79.5
70 and over	261	65	5	226	191	45	4	166.5
Total	1,485	141	186	1,321.5	1,158	92	77	1,073.5
				FEMALE				
Under 15	21	0	5	18.5	16	0	3	14.5
15–19	68	1	17	59	50	0	5	47.5
20–24	99	2	20	88	77	1	8	72.5
25–29	138	2	27	123.5	109	1	9	104
30–34	143	3	25	129	115	4	13	106.5
35–39	147	2	27	132.5	118	2	8	113
40–44	133	3	21	121	109	1	7	105
45–49	138	4	22	125	112	5	9	105
50–54	133	5	18	121.5	110	7	7	103
55–59	120	10	16	107	94	5	8	87.5
60–64	117	14	12	104	91	7	2	86.5
65–69	125	18	8	112	99	12	3	91.5
70 and over	384	86	6	338	292	62	3	259.5
Total	1,766	150	224	1,579	1,392	107	85	1,296

Table 5.2—Continued

Age	Number Starting 5th Year	5th Year		Years of Patient Care in 5th Year
		Deaths	Discharged	
MALE				
Under 15	31	0	3	29.5
15–19	44	1	3	42
20–24	70	1	5	67
25–29	72	2	4	69
30–34	73	2	5	69.5
35–39	76	2	3	73.5
40–44	80	1	4	77.5
45–49	78	0	2	77
50–54	82	5	2	78.5
55–59	86	6	7	79.5
60–64	84	7	7	77
65–69	71	13	0	64.5
70 and over	142	33	1	125
Total	989	73	46	929.5
FEMALE				
Under 15	13	0	2	12
15–19	45	0	4	43
20–24	68	2	2	66
25–29	99	1	1	98
30–34	98	2	4	95
35–39	108	1	5	105
40–44	101	3	4	97.5
45–49	98	4	4	94
50–54	96	4	4	92
55–59	81	7	1	77
60–64	82	8	1	77.5
65–69	84	9	1	79
70 and over	227	40	3	205.5
Total	1,200	81	36	1,141.5

[a] Rates from Malzberg, 1956, "Cohort Studies of Mental Disease in New York State, 1943 to 1949," *Mental Hygiene*, Vol. 40, Tables 5, 11.

labor force years lost. If the reader prefers, he may assume that our hypothetical population has the same distribution of mental disorder (and in the same intensity) as does Malzberg's population. Our assumption of the same rates of death and discharge seems to imply the latter assumption as well.

Given this assumption, it is easy to calculate the number of years of patient care in the first, second, third, fourth, and fifth years after admission. We simply apply the "correct" ratios to our hypothetical population and total the results. The results are presented in Table 5.2. In this table we show all computations for the first year in order that the reader better understand our method; for successive years beyond the first we show only the basic data. In all computations we assume that if an individual is discharged *during* a particular year, he receives one-half year of patient care.

The information provided in Table 5.2 can be summarized and the percentage of the maximum possible years of care calculated. This is done in Table 5.3.

Table 5.3—Maximum and Actual Years of Patient Care, Hypothetical Population, Male and Female

	First Year	Second Year	Third Year	Fourth Year	Fifth Year
Patients entering	10,000	6,180	3,251	2,550	2,189
Maximum years of care	10,000	6,180	3,251	2,550	2,189
Actual years of care	8,090	4,715	2,900	2,369	2,071
Per cent of maximum	80.9	76.3	89.2	92.9	94.6

A number of conclusions can be reached on the basis of the summaries provided in Table 5.3 and the data in Table 5.2. As can readily be seen, the savings in patient years of care occur chiefly in the first and second years. In the first year these savings occur because deaths are high (26 per cent of all first admissions), though discharges were lower

(12 per cent). The patient years "saved" in the second year result from high numbers of discharges (39 per cent of those starting the second year) though deaths were lower (8 per cent). During the third, fourth, and fifth years the percentage discharged (of those starting the year) fell to 13, 6, and 4 per cent respectively while deaths also were low (and falling): 9, 8, and 7 per cent respectively. Since relatively few patients died or were discharged after the second year, the actual number of years of care required was a high percentage of the maximum number possible for those years. We are unable to carry these calculations out beyond five years (this would be necessary to know the final total patient years of care needed), but we would expect that discharges would continue to decline while the relatively large number of young and middle-aged patients remaining (the older ones die in the first few years) would also bring a decline in the percentage dying. Both factors would probably imply many more years of patient care. In the five-year period following the first admissions, we could have expected that, as a very maximum, 5 times 10,000 years of patient care would be required. Instead of the 50,000 years of patient care, the entering group required only 20,146 years. This is 40 per cent of the maximum possible, a considerable saving.

Before translating these years of care and the savings into dollar terms, we will refine the data for the first year. As Malzberg points out (1956, p. 456), "Fourteen per cent of the first admissions were discharged during the first year. Within this period, most of the discharges occurred during the first three months. . . . There were relatively few discharges during the remainder of the first year of hospitalization." This suggests that we introduce some error when we assume that patients discharged during the first year spend a half-year in the hospital. The distribution of discharges during the first year is skewed to the left rather than symmetrical. It is possible to correct for this slight error since data are provided (for the first year) by quarters. A summary of the results of this correction is provided in Table 5.4.

Table 5.4—Maximum and Possible Quarter-Years of Patient Care During First Year of Hospitalization, Hypothetical Population, Male and Female

	First Quarter	Second Quarter	Third Quarter	Fourth Quarter	First Year Total
Patients entering	10,000	7,537	6,878	6,483	10,000
Maximum one-fourth years of care	10,000	7,537	6,878	6,483	40,000
Actual one-fourth years of care	8,768	7,208	6,680	6,336	28,992
Per cent of maximum	87.7	95.6	97.1	97.7	72.5

We thus find that breaking our first year of hospitalization into quarters (and assuming that individuals are discharged at the mid-point of the quarter) results in some modification of Table 5.3 and the answers derived therefrom. The required years of patient care in the first year drop from 8090 (81 per cent of the maximum) to 7248 (72 per cent of the maximum). The required years of patient care over the entire five-year period drop from 20,146 (40 per cent of the maximum) to 19,304 (39 per cent of the maximum).

The data on patient years of care needed can now be translated into dollar terms. We shall assume that the cost per patient year is $1190.32, the average for the United States in 1956 (Interstate Clearing House, 1956, Table 3). The breakdown of costs is given in Table 5.5.

Table 5.5—Costs of Patient Care During First Five Years After Hospitalization, Hypothetical Population

Time	COSTS (in thousands)			SAVINGS (in thousands)	
	Maximum Possible	Actual	Total	Due to Death	Due to Discharge
First three months	$ 2,976	$ 2,609	$ 366 [a]	$ 247	$ 119
Second three months	2,243	2,145	98	65	33
Third three months	2,047	1,988	59	42	17
Fourth three months	1,929	1,885	44	31	13
First year	9,195	8,627	567 [a]	385	182
Second year	7,356	5,612	1,743 [a]	296	1,447
Third year	3,870	3,452	417 [a]	173	244
Fourth year	3,035	2,820	214 [a]	118	96
Fifth year	2,606	2,465	141	92	49
Total	$26,062	$22,976	$3,082	$1,064	$2,018

[a] Differences due to rounding.

The maximum possible cost, had all 10,000 patients stayed in the hospital (no deaths or discharges), would have been $11,903,200 per year or $59,516,000 during the five-year period under consideration. The actual costs of $22,976,000 were 38.6 per cent of this total. The minimum cost if all patients were discharged within the first three months would have been $1,487,900.

It is felt that the data provided are useful in examining the impact of a group of first admissions since they incorporate both deaths and discharges. From the point of view of a hospital administrator, it is just as significant to know the savings in cost of patient care accruing from deaths as it is to know the savings resulting from discharge. The costs of patient care cannot be predicted without taking into account all factors that move patients out of the hospital.

The previous analysis provides results which may be utilized in a variety of ways. We can indicate one such use.

In 1954 there were a total of 3695 first admissions to public prolonged-care hospitals in Texas (U.S. Dept. of Health, Education, and Welfare, 1957, Part II, Table 7). We can make an estimate of the cost of care for this group of first admissions. We found that 10,000 first admissions required 19,304 years of patient care (at $1190.32 per patient year).

We must adjust our results for Texas both for the number of patients and the annual cost per patient. The 3695 Texas patients represent 7133 years of patient care. The cost per patient year in Texas was $756.39 in 1956 (Interstate Clearing House, 1956, Table 3). The cost for Texas during the first five years, i.e., 1954–1959, of the patients first admitted in 1954 can be expected to be about $5.4 million ($5,395,-329.87). This is clearly only an estimate, since the age and sex distribution of Texas patients may differ from that of New York State (1943–1949), and since patterns of patient care (and death and discharge rates) may differ.

There have also been striking changes in discharge rates since 1943–1949 with resulting declines in years of patient care needed, though these changes may be balanced by the fact that advances in medical science tend to reduce the death rate somewhat. We do not know the impact that these changes have on the cost picture. More recent cohort data would be required to assess their importance. In spite of such qualifications, it is felt that the approach utilized and the results achieved will be useful to those who must make some cost predictions and to those concerned with the impact of mental illness on the State budget and on the economy. Clearly, the results of the analysis should be revised as more and later data are made available.

DIRECT COSTS AS A FUNCTION
OF MENTAL DISORDER

We have analyzed the direct costs of patient care of a group of 10,000 patients with characteristics similar to those patients admitted to New York State mental institutions in the period 1943–1949. It is also possible to examine the costs of care for a group of patients with a given diagnosis. Many of the reservations we expressed earlier about the changes in discharge rates with time apply again. We turn for our basic data to the *Proceedings of the Second Conference of Mental Health Administrators and Statisticians,* Federal Security Agency, 1953, Appendix A, Table 9. In this table the patient years of care per 100 first admissions needed within the first year following admission are presented. The data refer to 1914 and to 1948 and the changes between these two dates are compared. We shall utilize the 1948 data only (Table 5.6).

Of course, we can easily adjust the results presented in Table 5.6 for changes in maintenance costs. In 1954, for example, the 540 patient years of care would have cost $642,600. These are the costs in the first year for the care received (540 patient years) by the 800 entering patients (100 in each diagnostic category). The approach utilized can be applied by any State interested in knowing what a given group of admissions in a particular diagnostic category will cost that State in the first year of hospitalization.

We have approached the problem of direct costs in two different ways. In our first analysis, we were concerned with a number of first admissions with a particular age and sex distribution (New York, 1943–1949). In our second approach we were concerned with a given number of first admissions

Table 5.6—Costs in First Year of Patient Years of Care Per 100 First Admissions, by Diagnosis, 1948

Diagnosis	Patient Years of Care Per 100 First Admissions Needed Within First Year Following Admission [a]	Cost of Care [b]
Schizophrenia	70.7	$ 46,591
Involutional psychosis	62.8	41,385
Alcoholic psychosis	62.5	41,188
Psychosis with mental deficiency	72.1	47,514
Manic-depressive psychosis	60.7	40,001
Syphilitic psychosis	71.3	46,987
Mental diseases of the senium [c]	70.9	46,723
All others [d]	69.0	45,471
Total	540.0	$355,860

[a] Patients discharged or dying were each credited with one-half patient year. Results based on unpublished data submitted by Arkansas, California, Louisiana, Michigan, Nebraska, Ohio, and Virginia.

[b] Based on a per capita maintenance cost in State hospitals in the United States in 1948 of $659.13.

[c] Includes psychoses with cerebral arteriosclerosis and senile psychosis.

[d] The conservative assumption has been made that per cents remaining in the hospital, on trial visit or discharged, and died from the above seven selected psychoses apply to psychotic first admissions with other or undiagnosed conditions and to nonpsychotic first admissions.

Source: Computed from Proceedings of the Second Conference, 1953, Appendix A, Table 9. Footnotes in original source (Footnote d has been shortened).

in various diagnostic categories. In both approaches we have calculated the costs of care for the given number of admissions (by age and sex, by diagnostic category). The answers obtained differ somewhat, but this is to be expected, since the base populations differ. Both approaches can be utilized in an examination of costs. (In our first approach 724.8 years of patient care are needed for the 1000 first admissions; our second approach requires 540 patient years for 800 admissions, equal to 600 for 1000 admissions divided equally by diagnostic category.)

DIRECT COSTS AS A FUNCTION OF AGE

The implications of our analysis are obvious. It is now possible to examine the impact that different age groups have on the costs of the mental hospital. Total costs over a period of time are a function both of the rate of death and discharge and of the number of admissions. Particular age groups may have large numbers of admissions but high death and discharge rates; other age groups may have few admissions but low death and discharge rates. It is useful to examine the costs as a function of age to see which age groups "create" the financial problems.

We shall proceed in the following manner:

1. Assume 1000 first admissions in each age group. Using death and discharge data (Malzberg, 1956) compute the number of years of patient care needed for the 1000 admissions, in the first year, second, third, fourth, and fifth years. We now know how many years of patient care each age group requires in the first five years of hospitalization.

2. But the number of individuals in each age group entering mental hospitals differ. Using 1954 first admissions data we shall multiply the years of hospitalization required per 1000 patients by the 1954 number of admissions divided by 1000. We now have the number of patient years of care required for the actual admissions in each age group.

3. The results of step 2 will be multiplied by the cost per patient year of hospitalization.

Table 5.7 indicates that, assuming equal numbers in each age group, the groups requiring the most years of care *in the first year* after hospitalization are ages 30–34 (males) and

Table 5.7—Years of Patient Care Needed in Each of First
Five Years of Hospitalization, by Age at Time
of Admission, Male and Female

Age	Number of Admissions	YEARS OF PATIENT CARE NEEDED DURING					Total
		First Year	Second Year	Third Year	Fourth Year	Fifth Year	
MALE							
Under 15	1,000	829	576	442	363	320	2,530
15–19	1,000	859	529	293	229	204	2,114
20–24	1,000	855	536	326	272	244	2,233
25–29	1,000	852	528	318	274	253	2,225
30–34	1,000	861	540	321	264	232	2,218
35–39	1,000	851	523	307	257	235	2,173
40–44	1,000	852	524	308	261	241	2,186
45–49	1,000	842	514	310	262	244	2,172
50–54	1,000	834	516	321	267	245	2,183
55–59	1,000	814	488	315	264	236	2,117
60–64	1,000	790	462	310	251	216	2,029
65–69	1,000	758	414	273	211	170	1,826
70 and over	1,000	675	284	188	136	99	1,382
Total	13,000	10,672	6,434	4,032	3,311	2,939	27,388
FEMALE							
Under 15	1,000	905	703	518	392	309	2,827
15–19	1,000	896	578	316	253	227	2,270
20–24	1,000	888	547	284	235	212	2,166
25–29	1,000	894	578	329	276	258	2,335
30–34	1,000	895	572	319	262	232	2,280
35–39	1,000	900	586	336	287	266	2,375
40–44	1,000	899	581	331	287	268	2,366
45–49	1,000	892	591	362	306	276	2,427
50–54	1,000	874	556	332	281	250	2,293
55–59	1,000	851	536	328	266	234	2,215
60–64	1,000	810	493	326	272	244	2,145
65–69	1,000	779	448	302	246	213	1,988
70 and over	1,000	707	336	227	174	137	1,581
Total	13,000	11,190	7,105	4,310	3,537	3,126	29,268
Grand total	26,000	21,862	13,539	8,342	6,848	6,065	56,656

Source: Based on data for New York State 1943–1949 (Malzberg, 1956).

under 15 (females). *Over the five-year period,* the most years of care are required by those under 15 (male and female). Although these patterns might change somewhat if we broke the first year into quarters (instead of assuming all deaths and discharges occur at the mid-point of the year) it is doubtful that this would materially affect the results.

We cannot predict the costs (or years of patient care) required after the first five years, but it is likely that these costs will be high for the younger age groups. This is the case because relatively few patients are discharged after five years, because death rates are low in those age groups, and because relatively large numbers of patients in the younger age groups arc still in the hospitals.

Table 5.8—Number of Patients Remaining in Hospitals After Five Years Out of 1000 Admissions in Each Age and Sex Group, by Age at First Admission and Sex

	NUMBER REMAINING		
Age	Male	Female	Total
Under 15	305	275	580
15–19	199	217	416
20–24	236	208	444
25–29	242	255	497
30–34	221	229	450
35–39	229	261	490
40–44	235	261	496
45–49	242	269	511
50–54	238	240	478
55–59	229	225	454
60–64	208	231	439
65–69	154	202	356
70 and over	90	124	214
Total	2,828 [a]	2,997 [a]	5,825

[a] Out of 13,000 original admissions.

The answer regarding costs of patient care, by age group, is quite clear in our hypothetical world of 1000 admissions per age group. We can multiply our "total" columns in Table 5.7 by the appropriate dollar cost per patient year of care and see which age group places the greatest burden on the budget. By reference to Table 5.8 we can obtain a rough idea of which particular age groups will be costly after the first five years.

In order to examine the impact of the 1954 admissions, by age group, we must now proceed as indicated previously in step (2). The results of this analysis are found in Table 5.9. We shall also compute the cost figures and incorporate them into Table 5.9.

In Table 5.9, based on United States first admissions (1954), we note that the costliest age groups are ages 25–44 for both males and females. This is true in spite of the fact that other age groups (under 15) require more years of care and that other age groups (70 and over) have about the same (male) or more (female) admissions. *The cost problem for hospitals lies in the 25–34 age group.*

In Chapter VI we shall analyze the impact on indirect costs of various diagnostic categories as a function of the age of first admissions. For a discussion of direct cost, however, it is sufficient at this point to examine costs as a function of age. The methods used in Chapter VI could be applied to the problem of direct costs as a function of mental disability.

Table 5.9, interestingly enough, permits us to assess the validity of our previous assumption (made in our earlier discussion of the New York 1943–1949 data) that the results in the early section of this chapter could be applied to the entire country (the reader will recall that we applied the results to Texas). We indicated that 10,000 first admissions distributed in relation to sex and age as were New York first

Table 5.9—Cost of Care in First Five Years Following Hospitalization, 1954 Admissions, by Age and Sex

MALE

Age	First Admissions	Years of Care Per 1000 Admissions	Years of Care for First Admissions	Cost of Care In First Five Years (in thousands)
Under 15	754	2,530	1,908	$ 2,271
15–24	5,616	2,174	12,209	14,533
25–34	9,690	2,222	21,531	25,629
35–44	10,552	2,180	23,003	27,381
45–54	8,826	2,178	19,223	22,882
55–64	6,234	2,073	12,923	15,383
65–70	3,223 [a]	1,826	5,885	7,005
70 and over	9,821	1,382	13,573	16,156
Total	54,716		110,255	$131,240

FEMALE

Age	First Admissions	Years of Care Per 1000 Admissions	Years of Care for First Admissions	Cost of Care In First Five Years (in thousands)
Under 15	427	2,827	1,207	$ 1,437
15–24	3,930	2,218	8,717	10,376
25–34	8,037	2,308	18,549	22,079
35–44	7,679	2,371	18,207	21,672
45–54	5,999	2,360	14,158	16,853
55–64	4,410	2,180	9,614	11,444
65–70	2,410 [a]	1,988	4,791	5,703
70 and over	8,456	1,581	13,369	15,913
Total	41,348		88,612	$105,477
Grand total	96,064		198,867	$236,717

[a] One-half of 65–74 age group.

Source: First admissions from *Patients in Mental Institutions,* 1954, Part II, Table 7. Cost figure from Interstate Clearing House, 1956, Table 3.

admissions 1943–1949 would require 19,304 years of patient care in the first five years after hospitalization. Using that ratio, we would find that the 96,064 United States first admissions (1954) would require 185,442 years of patient care (193,531 years if the first year is not divided into quarters). Table 5.9 indicates that 198,867 years are required. Some of the difference lies in the fact that the earlier approach broke the first year into quarters, yet even so the difference between the estimates is only 6.7 per cent (only 2.7 per cent if the quarterly adjustment for year one is omitted).

We also note from Table 5.9 that it is possible to obtain the total direct costs of care in the first five years for the United States of all first admissions (1954) without having to use our "standardized" results obtained earlier. (Those results are still useful for the United States in any other year and for individual States. They retain their general applicability because they are based on a standard 10,000 population.) The total direct costs for the first five years after hospitalization (1954–1959), based on an average annual cost per patient of $1190.32, would be $236,717,000 for the 96,064 patients with known age and an additional $56,039,000 for the 22,545 patients of unknown age (we assume these are distributed in the same way as those of known age). The total costs would, therefore, be $292,756,000.

SUMMARY

1. We have provided direct cost estimates (based on standard populations) as functions of age of admission and of diagnosis. These estimates can be applied to other populations in individual States or in the United States.

2. We have estimated the cost of care for 1954 first admissions during the period 1954–1959 to be near $300 million. This estimate would be changed if patterns of discharge or death are substantially different from those prevailing in New York State in the period 1943–1949.

VI

Significance of Indirect Costs

THE INDIRECT COSTS of mental illness were discussed in Chapter IV. At that time we estimated the loss to the economy caused by:

1. Patients resident in hospitals in a specific year.

2. First admissions to mental hospitals in their first year of hospitalization and over a period of time (various assumptions about length of stay were used to arrive at different estimates).

In those analyses we were concerned with arriving at estimates of losses, taking into account the age distribution of patients and of first admissions. This was required since we must know age before we can use the concept "expected working years," and before we can indicate the probability that a particular individual will or will not be in the labor force or will or will not be employed.

We shall now direct our attention to an examination of the impact that various diagnostic classifications have on *indirect* costs—i.e., which diagnostic categories are the "burdensome" ones to the economy, and which cause the greatest loss of working years. Tables 4.18 and 4.19 provided similar information on losses as a function of age for a male standard population and for the male 1954 first admissions. Tables 4.23 and 4.24 provided similar information for females. In those tables, we found that, of the total work years lost, the male age group 25–34 accounted for the largest percentage (in spite of the fact that there were more male first admissions in age group 35–44) and the same age group was also the "costliest" among females. We now examine the burden of indirect costs as a function of diagnostic category of mental illness. This, it is felt, will be useful in pointing up which mental disorders are the most expensive (in terms of indirect costs). We shall, as was done previously, make several simplifying assumptions. These will be spelled out so that the reader will know the foundation on which the analysis rests.

The problem we attempt to analyze can be posed as follows: Every year a number of patients enter public institutions for the mentally ill. These patients have various mental disorders. The years of patient care required depend on the mental disorders and the age distribution of the patients. Some mental disorders will require more care than others (see Chapter V, Table 5.6). It is, therefore, the case that some mental disorders will prove more burdensome to the economy, i.e., more work years will be lost. Since the number of expected work years is a function of age and since the age distribution in the various diagnostic categories differ, each diagnostic category will have its own "loss pattern." It is possible to see which mental disorder causes the greatest loss, dependent on (1) the number of admissions in the diagnostic categories and (2) the age distribution of admissions in each category.

The first step in any such analysis is to ascertain the total number of expected working years remaining for the patients in each diagnostic category. Although this task is a laborious one (in terms of the amount of calculation necessary), the logic of the approach is simple. We use the average expected working years, male and female, computed from Tables 4.11 and 4.12. Using one diagnostic group at a time, we multiply the number of first admissions in each age group by the expected working years for that age group and total our results to find the expected working years for all admissions.

To obtain the number of first admissions in each diagnostic category, we totaled the number of admissions in 1952 to State hospitals, county hospitals, psychopathic hospitals, and private hospitals as given in *Patients in Mental Institutions,* 1952, Part II, Tables 7, 10, 13 and Part III, Table 3. The method of computing the total expected working years is indicated in Table 6.1. Because the basic data are available in standard sources and because the computational tables are space consuming, we shall illustrate our detailed breakdown for only one diagnostic category. The reader will therefore find only the totals in Table 6.2.

We are now in a position to examine the implications of Table 6.2. Even before we examine the expected *losses* due to the various mental disorders, it is clear that (from the standpoint of working years) some disorders are much more important than others. Although it is true that the total expected working years (Column 3) depends in part on the number of admissions (Column 2), it also depends on the age distribution of the incoming patients. It is for that reason that we find various disorders with a high number of admissions and a relatively low number of expected working

Table 6.1—Detailed Computational Breakdown of Method Used to Calculate Expected Working Years, One Diagnostic Category, General Paresis, Male First Admissions, 1952

	Total Age Known	Under 15	15–24	25–34	35–44	45–54	55–64	65–74	75 and Over	Total Expected Working Years	Average Expected Working Years
(1) Institution											
State	1,338	—	32	85	313	422	315	143	28		
County	25	—	—	—	2	10	7	5	1		
Psychopathic	31	—	2	2	10	11	5	1	—		
Private	45	—	—	2	8	14	13	5	3		
Total	1,439	—	34	89	333	457	340	154	32		
(2) Av. Exp. Work Years	—	39	37	29	21	13	6	1	0		
(3) Total Exp. Work Years (1) × (2)	—	0	1,258	2,581	6,993	5,941	2,040	77[a]	0	18,890	13.1

[a] One-half of 154 × 1.

Table 6.2—Number of Expected Working Years Remaining, by Mental Disorder and Sex, All First Admissions, 1952

(1) Mental Disorder and Sex	(2) Number of Admissions (age known) [a]	(3) Expected Working Years	(4) Average Expected Working Years
With Psychosis			
General Paresis			
Male	1,439	18,890	13.1
Female	605	2,791	4.6
With other Forms of Syphilis of the C.N.S.			
Male	339	4,224	12.5
Female	196	874	4.5
With Epidemic Encephalitis			
Male	80	1,496	18.7
Female	56	427	7.6
With other Infectious Diseases			
Male	185	2,969	16.0
Female	115	814	7.1
Alcoholic			
Male	4,711	78,081	16.6
Female	1,218	7,370	6.1
Due to Drugs and other exogenous Poisons			
Male	350	5,741	16.4
Female	435	2,390	5.5
Traumatic			
Male	437	7,482	17.1
Female	126	780	6.2
With Cerebral Arteriosclerosis			
Male	9,772	19,394	2.0
Female	7,860	3,103	0.4
With Other Disturb. of Circulation			
Male	571	3,663	6.4
Female	432	1,262	2.9
With Convulsive Disorders			
Male	901	20,970	23.3
Female	771	6,035	7.8

(1) Mental Disorder and Sex	(2) Number of Admissions (age known) [a]	(3) Expected Working Years	(4) Average Expected Working Years
Senile			
Male	6,887	3,795	0.6
Female	8,344	556	0.1
Involutional Psychoses			
Male	2,334	19,180	8.2
Female	5,946	19,707	3.3
Due to Other Metabolic, etc., Diseases			
Male	334	3,519	10.5
Female	428	1,763	4.1
Due to New Growth			
Male	156	1,521	9.8
Female	130	631	4.9
Others with Organic Changes of the Nervous System			
Male	783	10,465	13.4
Female	647	2,776	4.3
Manic-Depressive			
Male	2,945	50,422	17.1
Female	5,283	34,055	6.4
Schizophrenia			
Male	13,929	368,522	26.5
Female	19,488	171,025	8.8
Paranoia and Paranoid Conditions			
Male	925	15,000	16.2
Female	1,067	5,411	5.1
With Psychopathic Personality			
Male	530	14,372	27.1
Female	327	3,107	9.5
With Mental Deficiency			
Male	1,212	32,804	27.1
Female	1,034	9,316	9.0
Other, Undiagnosed, and Unknown			
Male	1,460	27,115	18.6
Female	1,347	8,307	6.2

Table 6.2—Continued

(1) Mental Disorder and Sex	(2) Number of Admissions (age known) [a]	(3) Expected Working Years	(4) Average Expected Working Years
TOTAL			
Male	50,280	709,625	14.1
Female	55,855	282,500	5.1
Psychoneurosis			
Male	4,057	85,696	21.1
Female	7,304	55,238	7.6
Without Psychosis or Psychoneurosis			
Epilepsy			
Male	320	8,731	27.3
Female	219	2,257	10.3
Mental Deficiency			
Male	819	23,798	29.1
Female	574	6,056	10.6
Alcoholism			
Male	10,407	184,831	17.8
Female	2,119	13,490	6.4
Drug Addiction			
Male	816	17,732	21.7
Female	559	4,074	7.3
Personality Disorders Due to Epidemic Encephalitis			
Male	48	1,150	24.0
Female	15	128	8.5
Psychopathic Personality			
Male	1,759	46,803	26.6
Female	453	4,553	10.1
Primary Behavior Disorders			
Male	704	21,573	30.6
Female	513	5,669	11.1
Others and Unclassified			
Male	1,778	35,984	20.2
Female	942	6,392	6.8
TOTAL			
Male	16,651	340,602	20.5
Female	5,394	42,619	7.9

(1) Mental Disorder and Sex	(2) Number of Admissions (age known) [a]	(3) Expected Working Years	(4) Average Expected Working Years
Mental Disorder Undiagnosed			
Male	1,132	20,500	18.1
Female	711	4,692	6.6
No Mental Disorder Found			
Male	421	8,421	20.0
Female	284	1,902	6.7
TOTAL ALL PATIENTS [b]			
Male [c]	72,541	1,164,844	16.1
Female [d]	69,548	386,951	5.6

[a] From *Patients in Mental Institutions,* 1952, Part II, Tables 7, 10, 13; Part III, Table 3.
[b] Data do not include 294 Sex and Age unknown.
[c] Data do not include 8513 males age unknown.
[d] Data do not include 7450 females age unknown.

years (compare senility and involutional psychoses). In Column 4, the number of admissions plays no part; the age distribution of patients is all that matters. The relationships are shown in Table 6.3.

As can be seen from Tables 6.2 and 6.3, schizophrenia ranks first in number of admissions and total number of expected working years. This mental disorder is clearly most important. Alchoholism ranks second on both counts (male), but in spite of the fact that cerebral arteriosclerosis is third in admissions (male), psychoneurosis is third in total expected working years (this simply means that psychoneurosis has a younger age distribution than does cerebral arteriosclerosis).

If we knew nothing concerning treatment of mental illness, if, in other words, the patients who entered the hospital were never discharged, and if we were concerned only with indirect costs of various mental disorders, greatest research

Table 6.3—Rank of Number of Admissions, Expected and Average Working Years, by Mental Disorder and Sex

Mental Disorder	MALE Number of Admissions (Rank)	MALE Exp. Working Years (Rank)	MALE Aver. Exp. Working Years (Rank)	FEMALE Number of Admissions (Rank)	FEMALE Exp. Working Years (Rank)	FEMALE Aver. Exp. Working Years (Rank)
With Psychosis						
General Paresis	12	16	25	16	19	25
With other Forms of Syphilis of the C.N.S.	26	25	26	27	26	26
With Epidemic Encephalitis	31	31	14	31	31	10.5
With Other Infectious Diseases	29	29	23	30	27	13
Alcoholic	5	4	20	9	8	21
Due to Drugs and Other Exogenous Poisons	25	24	21	21	21	22
Traumatic	23	23	18.5	29	28	19.5
With Cerebral Arteriosclerosis	3	14	31	3	18	31
With Other Disturb. of Circulation	21	27	30	22	25	30
With Convulsive Disorders	16	12	9	13	11	9
Senile	4	26	32	2	30	32
Involutional Psychoses	8	15	29	5	4	29
Due to Other Metabolic, etc. Diseases	27	28	27	23	24	28
Due to New Growth	30	30	28	28	29	25
Others with Organic Changes of the Nervous System	19	20	24	15	20	27
Manic-Depressive	7	5	18.5	6	3	17.5
Schizophrenia	1	1	7	1	1	7
Paranoia and Paranoid Conditions	15	18	22	10	13	23
With Psychopathic Personality	22	19	4.5	24	17	5
With Mental Deficiency	13	8	4.5	11	6	6

	MALE			FEMALE		
Mental Disorder	Number of Admissions (Rank)	Exp. Working Years (Rank)	Aver. Exp. Working Years (Rank)	Number of Admissions (Rank)	Exp. Working Years (Rank)	Aver. Exp. Working Years (Rank)
Other Undiagnosed, and Unknown	11	9	15	8	7	19.5
Psychoneurosis	6	3	11	4	2	10.5
Without Psychosis or Psychoneurosis						
Epilepsy	28	21	3	26	22	3
Mental Deficiency	17	10	2	17	10	2
Alcoholism	2	2	17	7	5	17.5
Drug Addiction	18	17	10	18	16	12
Personality Disorders due to Epidemic Encephalitis	32	32	8	32	32	8
Psychopathic Personality	10	6	6	20	15	4
Primary Behavior Disorders	20	11	1	19	12	1
Others and Unclassified	9	7	12	12	9	14
Mental Disorder, Undiagnosed	14	13	16	14	14	16
No Mental Disorder Found	24	22	13	25	23	15

Source: Table 6.2.

emphasis should be devoted to schizophrenia (and to the other mental disorders in accordance with their rank in total expected working years) since that is where the greatest losses and, consequently, potential savings lie.

It is in this sense that we would argue that Table 6.3 is extremely significant. It helps provide a rational economic basis for the allocation of research expenditures. Although we would not suggest that the types of information presented in Tables 6.2 and 6.3 should be the sole criteria in determining the uses to which research funds should be put, we would put forth the idea that when resources are limited, they should be economized and devoted to the most serious problems (economic and human).

Our data provides some of the types of information that can be used in judging the relative economic seriousness of various problems. Implicit in this approach is the assumption that equal research sums can yield results on a variety of problems. If one knows in advance that relatively small expenditures can bring fruitful results in small areas, it may still be advisable to tackle the small problems. Our data are only one side of the coin. Intelligent estimates about the probability of research success and the kinds of expenditures that might bring such success are still required. It may, however, be that one does not know in advance of the research which areas might prove most fruitful. If that is the case, the assumption of equal probability of success may be used.

It is now possible to apply estimates on per cent of working years lost (Malzberg, 1950) to the data we have gathered. We know the total number of expected working years by mental disorder, and if we multiply these figures by the estimated per cent of working years lost we shall obtain an estimate of the total number of working years lost (by mental disorder). Our approach is, therefore, similar to that used in Chapter IV, where we first assumed patients are not discharged from the mental hospital and then relaxed that assumption. The results of the analysis are presented in Table 6.4.

Although we argued previously that the total *expected* working years should be considered if one wanted to allocate research money wisely, the reader will recall that this was based on the assumption that patients stayed in the hospital once admitted. Under such conditions the major problem

Table 6.4—Estimated Loss of Working Years, First Admissions, by Mental Disorder and Sex, 1952

Estimated Loss of Working Years

Mental Disorder	Per Cent	TOTAL Males	TOTAL Females	AVERAGE Males	AVERAGE Females
General Paresis	70	13,223	1,954	9.2	3.2
With Other Syphilis of the C.N.S.	60	2,534	524	7.5	2.7
With Epidemic Encephalitis	75	1,122	320	14.0	5.7
With Other Infectious Diseases	40	1,188	326	6.4	2.8
Alcoholic	50	39,040	3,685	8.3	3.0
Due to Drugs and Other Exogenous Poisons	50	2,870	1,195	8.2	2.7
Traumatic	50	3,741	390	8.6	3.1
With Cerebral Arteriosclerosis	85	16,485	2,638	1.7	0.3
With Other Disturbances of Circulation	40	1,465	505	2.6	1.2
With Convulsive Disorders	85	17,824	5,130	19.8	6.7
Senile	95	3,605	528	0.5	0.1
Involutional	60	11,508	11,824	4.9	2.0
Due to Other Metabolic, etc. Diseases	40	1,408	705	4.2	1.6
Due to New Growth	95	1,445	599	9.3	4.6
With Organic Changes of Nervous System	70	7,326	1,943	9.4	3.0
Manic-Depressive	40	20,169	13,622	6.8	2.6
Dementia Praecox	65	239,539	111,166	17.2	5.7
Paranoia and Paranoid Conditions	75	11,250	4,058	12.2	3.8
With Psychopathic Personality	50	7,186	1,554	13.6	4.8
With Mental Deficiency	10	3,280	932	2.7	0.9
Psychoneuroses	40	34,278	22,095	8.4	3.0

Source: Per cent from Malzberg, B., 1950, "Mental Illness and the Value of A Man," Mental Hygiene, 34, Table 1. Totals arrived at by applying per cent to Column 3, Table 6.2; averages by dividing Totals by Column 2, Table 6.2

would indeed be the particular mental disorder involving the greatest total working years. That assumption can now be relaxed; some of the mental health problems have already been solved (at least in part).

Table 6.4 provides us with information about working years *lost*, i.e., about the problem of mental illness as it exists today. This table, therefore, provides an even better basis on which to judge expenditures. It should, however, be pointed out once again that our calculations cannot provide all the answers to the relevant questions, for we have had to abstract from various considerations. The loss for females is, for example, an understatement of the magnitude of the problems involved. We have dealt with the loss in working years and have, therefore, excluded the female as mother and housewife. This clearly ignores the services that many females perform.

Table 6.5—Rank of Loss of Expected Working Years, First Admissions, by Mental Disorder and Sex, 1952

| | Rank of Estimated Working Years | | | |
| | TOTAL | | AVERAGE | |
Mental Disorder	Male	Female	Male	Female
General Paresis	7	9	8	7
With Other Syphilis of the C.N.S.	16	17	13	13.5
With Epidemic Encephalitis	21	21	3	2.5
With Other Infectious Diseases	20	20	15	12
Alcoholic	2	7	11	10
Due to Drugs and Other Exogenous Poisons	15	12	12	13.5
Traumatic	12	19	9	8
With Cerebral Arteriosclerosis	6	8	20	20
With Other Disturbances of Circulation	17	18	19	18
With Convulsive Disorders	5	5	1	1
Senile	13	16	21	21
Involutional	8	4	16	16
Due to Other Metabolic, etc. Diseases	19	14	17	17
Due to New Growth	18	15	7	5
With Organic Changes of Nervous System	10	10	6	10
Manic-Depressive	4	3	14	15
Dementia Praecox	1	1	2	2.5
Paranoia and Paranoid Conditions	9	6	5	6
With Psychopathic Personality	11	11	4	4
With Mental Deficiency	14	13	18	19
Psychoneuroses	3	2	10	10

Source: Table 6.4.

Table 6.6—Working Years Lost Through Prolonged Illness-Absenteeism, by Disability

Disability	Rate Per 1,000 Employed	Number Affected	Weeks Lost (Average)	Years Lost (Total)
MALES (42,377,000 Employed)				
Diseases of the Digestive System	7	296,639	8.5	50,429
Diseases of the Circulatory System	4	169,508	11.9	40,343
Accidents, Poisonings and Violence	3	127,131	10.7	27,206
Diseases of the Bones and Organs of Movement	2	84,754	12.3	20,849
Infective and Parasitic Diseases	1	42,377	21.9	18,561
Diseases of the Respiratory System	2	84,754	9.0	15,256
Mental, Psychoneurotic and Personality Disorders	1	42,377	16.7	14,154
Neoplasms	1	42,377	12.8	10,849
Allergic, Endocrine System, Metabolic and Nutritional Disorders	1	42,377	12.3	10,425
Diseases of the Nervous System and Sense Organs	1	42,377	11.7	9,916
Diseases of the Genito Urinary System	1	42,377	10.3	8,730
FEMALES (18,861,000 employed)				
Diseases of the Genito-Urinary System	9	169,749	10.2	34,269
Diseases of the Digestive System	8	150,888	9.5	28,669
Accidents, Poisonings and Violence	5	94,305	11.3	21,313
Diseases of the Circulatory System	4	75,444	10.6	15,994
Diseases of the Bones and Organs of Movement	3	56,583	11.4	12,901
Neoplasms	3	56,583	10.9	12,335
Diseases of the Respiratory System	4	75,444	7.9	11,920
Mental, Psychoneurotic and Personality Disorders	2	37,722	13.4	10,110
Allergic, Endocrine System, Metabolic, and Nutritional Disorders	2	37,722	11.9	8,978
Infective and Parasitic Diseases	1	18,861	13.9	5,243
Diseases of the Blood and Blood-Forming Organs	1	18,861	11.5	4,338
Diseases of the Nervous System and Sense Organs	1	18,861	10.6	3,998
Deliveries and Complications of Pregnancy, Childbirth and the Puerperium	1	18,861	10.0	3,772
Diseases of the Skin and Cellular Tissue	1	18,861	7.9	2,980

Source: Computed from data in Research Council for Economic Security, Prolonged Illness-Absenteeism.

Whereas our data have relevance for the economy, they tend to underestimate the impact that mental illness has on the female and on the family. It would not be warranted, therefore, to conclude that the problem of mental illness among females, or the impact of mental illness on females, is minor, even though it is true that the impact on *working* females is of relatively small consequence (if only because there are relatively few working females).

Before concluding our discussion of indirect costs and their significance, we should like to turn to the comparison of mental illness and other disabilities. In this comparison we utilize the data on prolonged illness-absenteeism gathered by the Research Council for Economic Security. As indicated previously (Chapter IV), these data understate the significance of total mental illness (since very long-term care data are probably not given their real weight), but within the limits of the data the results are revealing. The data are presented in Table 6.6.

SUMMARY

1. We have calculated the indirect cost (in terms of expected working years) for various diagnostic categories of mental illness. These costs, as shown, depend on the number of admissions and the age distribution of admissions. The results of the analysis provide a measure of the burden of various mental disorders.

2. We have compared working years lost in prolonged illness-absenteeism for various disabilities. This provides some standards of comparison for mental illness and other illnesses.

VII

Conclusions

THE STUDY has been concerned with the direct and with the indirect costs of mental illness. In Chapters III, IV, V, and VI we have attempted to measure these costs and assess their importance. Each of these chapters contains its own summary and we shall, therefore, devote major attention in these concluding remarks to a discussion of the meaning and implications of the results.

Mental illness, as has been shown, is expensive. Our results, in dollar terms, large as they are, understate the full costs by significant amounts because they do not include *all* of the impact that *all* mental illness has. Adequate data on that significant portion of mental illness among patients not reaching the mental hospitals is, at present, lacking. Were complete data available in that area, the measurable impact of mental illness would be materially increased. Continued study of these and other similar problems is certainly warranted. In spite of these qualifications, and in spite of the fact that no undertaking of this sort is ever really "completed," the data obtained can serve as a basis for various conclusions. Let us, therefore, spell out some of the implications of the results.

We start with the fact that mental health is *expensive*. It is clearly a burden upon the individual States and their budgets. Even aside from the substantial investment the States have made in plant and equipment, the maintenance expenditures for public mental hospitals were 3.06 per cent of State general revenues (1950 data, U.S. Public Health Service, 1952, Table 2).

It accounts for a considerable part of Veterans Administration expenditures on hospital care and on pensions and compensation.

Although—because so much public free care is provided—mental illness may not account for a high percentage of private medical expenses in any given year, the long-term nature of much of mental illness suggests that total private cost per patient *as time passes* may be significant (as compared with total cost *as time passes* of other illnesses). The long-term nature of mental illness suggests, furthermore, that the burdens placed on the family by loss of income and the total indirect costs of mental illness are considerable.

Whereas it would be both interesting and useful (for purposes of allocating research funds, for example) to compare the total direct and indirect costs of mental illness with the total costs of other illnesses, we have refrained from so doing. The temptation is to include such comparisons, but there is great danger in doing this. The danger, of course, lies in the fact that without a full study of the costs of other illnesses, one would have to rely on published figures from official and semi-official (from public and private) bodies. There is no doubt that some of the published figures are reliable (there is also no doubt that some are extremely unreliable), but it is impossible to assess their reliability without analysis of the methods used in arriving at the estimates.

The large differences between the estimates contained in this study and some of the popular estimates of the costs of mental illness certainly bear witness to the fact that one should approach published data on costs with a high degree of caution. Our strictures on this subject can, however, be made more general. The difficulty lies not only in the reliability of the data (i.e., whether or not gross errors in logic, double counting, etc. have been made), but also in the fact that data measure different things.

The reader will recall that we arrived at a number of different cost estimates in our earlier chapters. These estimates, based on different assumptions, measured different "costs." When properly qualified, no one estimate was any more or less correct than any other estimate; they simply estimated different costs. It is clear, however, that we could not simply compare published cost estimates of other illnesses with our own results without studying the various illnesses closely in order to be able to judge which of our estimates, if any, were arrived at in the same way and which start with the same assumptions as the ones with which the comparison is made. If data even *within* the field of mental illness are not standardized, how much worse it must be when we examine a variety of illnesses. It is for these reasons that we must guard against the natural inclinations to compare just for the sake of comparison, even if we do not know what it is we are comparing.

Even without *inter*-illness comparisons, it is still clear that in mental illness and health we are dealing with a disability that has large direct costs. This should not suggest that the desirable thing is to eliminate or minimize these direct costs.[1] Yet there is the danger that the use of the term "costs" may imply such a program, at least to some people. "Costs," after all, we are commonly told, are undesirable. It is patently obvious that this is not the case.

Any business firm, for example, could eliminate its costs by the simple expedient of "going out of business" (merely stopping production would not be sufficient since "fixed" costs continue). Yet few do so (at least voluntarily). What is desired, from the producer's standpoint, is that costs be minimized *consistent with a given level of production*. One would not quarrel with this concept. If the same end can be achieved in two ways, one of which requires less input, then clearly that way is "better"—i.e., more desirable. Similarly, it would generally be agreed that this principle has application outside the business world.

Although it would be dangerous indeed to suggest that nonprofit and governmental units should be "run like business," there are certain economic principles that have a general applicability. Among these principles we can include the one we cite: that resources be conserved and utilized efficiently. The difficulty in applying this principle lies, of course, in the fact that the real world is dynamic rather than static and that it is extremely difficult in the nonprofit sector of the economy to define the end being achieved, to know how to alter the desired end over time, and above all to recognize when wise (in an economic sense) expenditures are being made.

Nor should the nonprofit sector operate only as if its aim *is* to make a profit, and then, as a final "accounting" step, adjust rates (or expenditures) so that no profit shows. To do so is to miss what we believe is the essence of the non-profit institution, its philosophy, its purpose. The hospital that lowers its patient charges to eliminate the profit that might arise (would that hospitals were in *this* financial predicament!) may have forgotten its purpose of caring for the sick. The university that eliminates its profit may still not have done enough; its purpose is not only to run a no-profit, no-loss institution but to spread knowledge.

What we are suggesting is merely that public institutions must remember the purposes for which they were set up and that they should not congratulate themselves and feel that they are accomplishing these purposes merely because they do not make a profit. Economic and budgetary problems and principles are, therefore, not the only guiding principles for the institutions that society has established for the ultimate purpose of supporting, caring for, and advancing the members of that society and the society itself.

Yet, once the above qualification has been made, the fact remains that economic and budgetary considerations do have a role to play, even if it is not the sole role; the further fact remains that when resources are scarce (as they always are)—and with other, e.g., humanitarian, considerations being equal—the program that can "make an economic case for itself" has some advantage over the program that is unable to do so. What type of economic case can a welfare program argue? In particular, what economic reasoning can those concerned with mental illness bring before the public?

The first and foremost point, it seems to the author, is the recognition that the concept of total costs as comprising both direct and indirect costs is the only meaningful concept. Once it is clear that we must deal with total cost, it is also clear that costs (in this sense) cannot be eliminated. Surely we all agree that direct costs can be decreased in a variety of ways, e.g., by elimination of existent programs or even obscuring of problems. This, however, does not eliminate total costs and may not (indeed, probably does not) reduce them. We can do no better than to quote Leon H. Keyserling who, when appearing as Chairman of the Council of Economic Advisers before the President's Commission on the Health Needs of the Nation, stated, "First, I assume that the cost to a nation of illness exists whether we deliberately finance that cost or not. In other words, if a part of our population suffers from ill health needlessly, the Nation bears that cost regardless of whether or not it decides to finance that cost" (The President's Commission, 1952, Vol. IV, p. 125).

The problem is, therefore, not as complex as it would be if we asked, "Should we bear the *direct* costs of mental illness?" and did not consider total costs at all. By itself, this question is partly a humanitarian and partly an economic question and is, therefore, "complex." When viewed from the perspective of total cost, more dimensions are added and the problem becomes *simpler*.

The economist *qua* economist (abstracting from the other considerations that impel him and other members of society) would hasten to point out that it may be that the answer to the question does not even involve humanitarian and ethical value judgements on which differences of opinion may exist but can be answered on economic grounds alone. It may be that the answer is really quite simple: that increases in direct costs reduce *total* costs (it may, as we shall point out later, even be true that increases in direct costs in the short run may reduce *direct* costs in the long run). What we are saying is that Chapters IV and VI on indirect costs were not included in this study as an aside but are an integral part of the consideration of the economic impact of mental illness. These costs are as much a burden to the Nation as are the more obvious costs discussed in Chapters III and V. To reduce direct costs without considering the impact on indirect costs is to adopt a limited and dangerous perspective.

This is not to suggest that the problem of allocation of resources is not a real problem. It is, but only in a static sense. It is still true that we must ask whether we should devote our resources (manpower, capital equipment, other) to this program or to that program, to housing or to education, to highways or to hospitals. But the problem may lie not in the use to which a fixed amount of resources are to be put, but rather in how to increase these resources.

We may have the best of all possible worlds, a world in which the using of resources in a particular way does not come (in a dynamic sense) at the expense of any other uses, but instead increases the total supply of resources available. An increase in the number of psychiatrists, for example, may not—in the long run—mean a decrease in the number of people employed in other areas of economic activity but rather an *increase* in the total labor force. Nor is it "utopian" to suggest that this best of all possible worlds exists. This is the world we face in the area of education. Is not one of the compelling economic arguments for education that the resources devoted to education are not a cost but an "investment," that we will increase the quality of the labor force in such a way as to reap benefits far exceeding the costs—i.e., that an educated labor force minus the manpower in the field of education can produce more than an uneducated labor force plus the manpower previously devoting itself to education?

The question at this point must therefore be, "Does this best of all possible worlds prevail in the field of mental illness?" Is it merely logically possible for such conditions to exist (i.e., that increased expenditures on the care of those mentally ill will reduce the indirect costs by more than the direct expenditures were increased) or will this really happen? The study has not attempted to find an answer to this question. Conflicting evidence exists and it would be a major undertaking to examine various experiments carefully enough to be certain of the results. Some would argue that more expensive therapy results in much higher rates of discharge; others would suggest that changes in therapy (i.e., new techniques, drugs, etc.), changes that do not necessarily involve greater expenditures, can account for the recent increase in discharge rates; still others state that increased rates of discharge (in the first year of hospitalization) may be due to earlier hospitalization. We would not presume to comment on this subject without undertaking the type of close examination that this problem calls for. Although we do not, therefore, suggest the answer to the question we raised at the beginning of this paragraph, we do suggest that the answer is worth seeking.

There is another type of direct expenditure (cash outlay) that also impinges on indirect costs and that may, if increased, result in a lowering of indirect costs and of total costs (indeed, even of other direct costs for care). We refer to expenditures on research. Difficulties in assessing the benefits of *future* research are of a different order than the difficulties in assessing the value of increased expenditures on patient care. Whereas the latter can presumably be investigated with the use of control experiments, etc., the former is by its very nature unpredictable.

No control experiment can tell us *today* what success (if any) will crown today's and tomorrow's research endeavors. We have every right to assume that investment in research will advance knowledge and provide beneficial results, but we cannot predict what the knowledge or results will be. He would be foolish, indeed, who would dare guarantee any given results for a given amount of money. Although all this is true, historical precedent suggests that, though any one individual piece of research is a "gamble," this is not true of research in general. There is, of course, no guarantee that because research has yielded fruitful results in the past it will do so in the future, but there is certainly presumptive evidence that this is the case. And that research in general and in mental illness in particular has indeed yielded results in the past seems to be evident. Although we shall not document so obvious a case, we can refer the reader to Malzberg (1950), Horatio M. Pollock, *Mental Diseases and Social Welfare* (1941) and to Federal Security Agency, 1953, for types of information useful in this area.

It can certainly be accepted that research may bring beneficial results, although some might wonder whether the particular problem is important and significant enough to justify spending moneys even if a solution were guaranteed. Even if we were to base our judgment on economic data alone (and we would *not* do so), this is clearly the case with mental illness. The data in Chapters III and IV—data that suggest that the annual direct and indirect costs add up to $2.4 billion at the very minimum—document the fact that the problem is large enough and the benefits accruing to society, if it were solved, are significant enough to justify sizable expenditures on research. When we consider the long-run impact (over time) of indirect costs, it is even more apparent that our economy stands to gain much if even only slight inroads were made into the problem.

We have discussed the concept of *total* costs, have emphasized that direct and indirect costs are closely tied together, and have suggested that it may be true that an increase in direct expenditures (costs) may reduce indirect costs appreciably. The fact remains, however, that governmental units may be concerned that the direct costs are borne by the State (or Federal) budget while the benefits (reduction of indirect and total costs) accrue to society. They may be inclined to feel that "all this is well and good from the standpoint of society but it doesn't solve the government's budgetary problem." Where shall these increases in expenditure come from?

The author feels that the question is irrelevant. It is clear to him that government should not hesitate to spend funds if it can be shown that these funds will bring a net gain to society (and especially when there is both a human and an economic gain). Yet this type of question recurs so frequently that it may not be sufficient (and is probably not convincing) to dismiss it as "irrelevant."

In order to respond to the question in an *economic* framework we therefore suggest that the answer to the problem lies in the fact that if the positive results hoped for are achieved, the governmental budget, too, will be assisted. An individual in a mental institution contributes nothing to the income of the State (he pays no income tax). If that individual is returned to society and becomes a wage earner, an employed member of the labor force, he will contribute to the general revenues of the State by the payment of taxes. Although the tax payments in any given year may not equal the increased expenditures it took to bring the individual back into the labor force, it must be remembered that the tax payments continue year after year whereas the expenditure is (hopefully) a one time occurrence. Intensive study of discharged patients would be necessary before we could be certain that the tax payments are really significant. This would depend on the work and income patterns of discharged patients. For the present we must be satisfied with the statement that this *may* be the case, that the situation may not be as dark as is sometimes suggested.

We now shift our emphasis somewhat from a consideration of the indirect cost benefits to the economy if an individual is returned to society to a consideration of the impact of direct expenditures in the short run on direct expenditures in the long run. Again the data presented in Chapter V have relevance.

Clearly total direct costs per patient are high, and the more so if the patient is relatively young and stays in the hospital for a number of years. Large savings can, therefore, accrue to the governmental unit (and ultimately to the taxpayer) if patients can be discharged sooner. Such savings have indeed occurred over time (the reader is again referred to the citations we mentioned earlier, e.g., Malzberg, Pollock). It should be clear, however, that we say "large savings," not "decreased expenditures." We do not suggest that increased expenditures today *will* mean decreased expenditures tomorrow. We shall explore some of the reasons behind this qualification subsequently.

For the present we contend that the savings which may accrue, though they may not mean that expenditures may be reduced in future years, do mean that expenditures may be less than they would otherwise have been. It may be that the indirect costs cannot be eliminated, that the individual even if discharged may not return to the labor force and to the ranks of the employed. Even so, and again abstracting from the human values which suggest that it is desirable aside from the monetary considerations advanced herein to cure and discharge a person, the governmental unit would find that discharges mean considerable savings (particularly when capital construction costs are considered).

In a larger sense, it may prove to be the case that increased expenditures on programs that bring the person into the hospital as early as possible (or that make it unnecessary for him to enter the hospital) may yield the largest savings of all (again, savings over what might have been; *not* necessarily reduced expenditures). Certainly there is evidence that many individuals believe that State expenditures, though large, are much smaller today than they would have been had discharge rates not increased in recent years. For example:

Prior to 1955 the rolls of the mentally ill in our state hospitals had been increasing by about 2400 patients each year. In 1955 a broad program of intensified treatment including the expanded use of new tranquilizing drugs was put into effect. The results are impressive. During 1955-56, 23 per cent more patients were released than in the preceding year. This improved rate has been maintained ever since.

The increase in the number of patients released is reflected in a reduction in hospital populations, amounting to 450 patients in 1955–56 and 470 in 1956–57. In addition to the incalculable human benefits which this reversal of the prior trend represents, it has also meant that the state has been saved a very large amount of additional cost.

Had the earlier rising trend continued, we would have been faced by 1959 with increased construction needs of some $170,000,-000 and increased maintenance costs of nearly $10,000,000 annually (Governor Harriman's annual message to the New York State Legislature, 1958).[2]

We indicated earlier that it was important to distinguish between reductions in expenditures (an absolute decline in dollars spent) and savings in expenditures (an expenditure that is less than the expenditure that would have been required). This distinction is important. It would be incorrect and misleading to suggest that increases in expenditures today, even if these increased expenditures resulted in significant increases in the discharge rates, would necessarily lead to a reduction in *direct* costs in the future. Although such a hope would be comforting indeed, it may be false. The reasons why this might not be the case are twofold:

1. At the same time that advances in the treatment of mental illness increase the discharge rate and, therefore, tend to reduce the number of resident patients, advances in general medicine may result in extensions of the life expectancy of elderly people (including those in mental institutions) thus tending to increase the number of resident patients (and in any case extending the number of years those who are not discharged spend in the hospital). We do

not know which of these opposite tendencies would prevail.

2. It may be that public knowledge about increasingly successful hospital care (combined, possibly, with higher costs of private care) will bring more individuals into the mental hospitals. The demand for medical services is in part a function of the availability of these services and of their quality. To the extent that the rate of discharges from mental institutions shows a marked increase, it is possible that people will avail themselves of the services provided to an even greater degree than heretofore. The better the quality of medical care available, the more willing the public may be to have this care.

This *may,* in part, mean a substitution of State provided services for personal medical care. In all probability, this substitution would be rather small and might be accompanied by an increase in the absolute amounts paid to hospitals by the patients themselves. To the observer this increase in direct costs might *appear* as an increase in the total costs of mental illness. This appearance would be deceiving. All that would be happening would be that relatively hidden personal costs would be brought into the open. To the extent, however, that increased admissions would come from groups and individuals previously not spending significant sums on personal care, there would, indeed, be an increase in the direct costs (over what would be spent if previous admission rates continued).

The increased admissions that we hypothesize would not, however, imply an increase in *indirect* costs (unless the availability of resources led individuals who were well to consider themselves sick). If the individuals who comprise the increased admissions were previously sick, their residence in the hospital would not alter the indirect costs of mental illness. Indeed, it is possible that the indirect costs would decrease as a result of increased admissions and quicker and higher recovery rates. The decrease in indirect costs would tend to reduce the total costs of mental illness.[3] Again we must remember that society must be concerned with both indirect and direct costs. Measures which reduce indirect costs, though they may add to direct costs, are to be welcomed. Were this not the case, then it would make sense from an economic point of view to ignore the whole problem of mental illness, since by so doing we could reduce direct costs substantially. This could hardly be called "progress."

The final question that we must discuss is: "What *can* society afford to spend on mental illness?" Many of our earlier remarks have suggested the kinds of economic considerations that should be involved in an answer (by society) to the question, "What *should* society spend on mental illness?" The economist cannot answer the first question.

An economy can afford to spend whatever it desires to spend. All that is necessary in order to spend more on one thing is that we spend less on something else. We would have to give up something (*in the short run*) if expenditures on mental illness were increased (as pointed out previously, the long-run situation might be far different). It is not for us to suggest the "proper" allocation of tax money, nor is it our place to suggest what the tax rate should be.

What society can spend (and ultimately what society should spend) depends on the value system that society holds to. It is obvious that society *can* spend much more on mental illness (or on anything) than it presently is doing. Whether or not it chooses to do so is another question.

We can provide data to assist us in understanding the implications of additional expenditures, the economic benefits to be derived therefrom, the gains, the costs. These may *aid in answering* the question, "What *should* society do?" They do not *answer* the question. The answer is up to society. The question, "What *can* society do?" cannot be answered.

Our data suggest that the problem of mental illness is significant enough so that the question might well be put: "What can society afford *not* to spend on mental illness and health?" We can do nothing; we can do much. Our value system will decide which course we choose. The economic data raise the question whether we dare do nothing.

In the preceding pages in this chapter we have discussed some of the economic issues that are implied in the data presented in the body of the report. Although we do not intend to summarize the statistical data, it is clear that the issues we discuss are ultimately dependent on the data themselves.

The study has provided some of the information on which policy decisions must be based. It is hoped that it has also succeeded in providing an outline of a method to be used in this type of research. If we have been successful in the latter endeavor, it will be possible to utilize new data as they become available and thus to amend the results obtained herein. To do so and to analyze the problem touched on but not investigated would be fruitful and necessary if further knowledge and progress is to be made.

The nature of statistics is that they become outdated.

The nature of research is that it often raises as many questions as it answers.

Mental illness is a problem of sufficient magnitude to warrant continued economic research in order to provide as current and complete data as possible and in order to answer the unanswered questions.

Notes

1. Should mental illness be eliminated (or only reduced) the task of maintaining full employment would be made more difficult. This challenge would, it is hoped, be willingly accepted by the economist. Although the economist's task is made easier by the fact that sick people are not in the labor force and thus, by definition, not unemployed, it is to be wished that medical research will not permit the economist to "pat himself on the back" but will continue to spur him on by making his problem ever more difficult.

2. Earnings on investments would, presumably, continue even after death. It is for this reason that we refer to wage and salary rather than money income.

3. The family would also be "better off" economically if a young child dies, but only if it is assumed that the child's future earnings would not be contributed to the family (more correctly, if the present value of that part of his future earnings that are contributed to the family is less than the present value of the future expenditures on the child). It may be that the elderly parent or child not only add pleasure to the family unit but also create a situation wherein the breadwinner, happy rather than despondent, works to his maximum capabilities. With the death

of the parent or child the breadwinner's economic efforts fall off, and it can be said that the parent or child thus, indirectly, has economic value. Such situations cannot be measured and are ignored. It is assumed that the breadwinner's economic activities remain the same.

4. The actual calculation is more complex than this because of the differences in output by males and females. To take account of this difference, Mr. Reynolds assigns a proportionality factor to males and females based on their weekly earnings. The average output per male thus is equal to the net product times the average male weekly earnings divided by the sum of the number of working males times the male average weekly earnings plus the number of working females times the female average weekly earnings. The average output per female differs in only one way; the net product is multiplied by average *female* weekly earnings. The ratio of average output per male to average output per female is, therefore, equal to the ratio of weekly earnings per male to weekly earnings per female (Reynolds, 1956, p. 397).

5. Although one may express some doubts about the usefulness of marginal productivity theory in a world of monopsonistic buyers of labor services and monopolistic sellers, in a world of "bigness," the logic of the approach remains. In a world of big labor and big business the wage may, indeed, not be exactly equal to marginal revenue product—and this, not only because of the difficulties of estimating the latter. They should, however, tend toward equality. While we may entertain some doubts about the empirical measurements we remain wedded to the logic of the approach and suggest that this is the best approach for our purposes. Closely allied to the marginal productivity theory is the law of diminishing returns. This suggests that the wage rate would decline somewhat if those who are mentally ill were added to the labor force and found employment. The decline would result from the fact that as these individuals were added to other factors of production which are fixed in the short run, their productivity would be less than that of the individuals previously employed. We ignore this

consideration because it cannot be measured and is of a short run nature in any case.

6. Reynolds (1956) imputes an output to the housewife equal to the output of the working woman. Although this is in line with his calculation of "average expectation of working life (as worker and housewife)," it does mean that one should recalculate "net domestic product at factor cost" using this new measure. If this is not done the "unrealized output" appears as a much larger percentage of the net product than it should. We would face the same problem of recalculating National Income if housewives' services were given a money value.

CHAPTER III

1. The average daily census of patients in government non-Federal mental institutions showed a decline in 1956. The number of beds available also declined (*Hospitals*, 1957, p. 355). Much evidence exists, however, to indicate that additional expenditures are required to bring existing facilities up to "standard."

2. Since, in general, governmental accounting units do not include depreciation, and value their capital assets at original cost, one might assume that changes in total assets as shown in Table 3.5 represent changes in gross value of plant and equipment. This suggests that increases in total assets occur when expenditures are made on new capital equipment or on the expansion or renovation of existing facilities. If this be the case it would imply that about 1.4 billion dollars were spent in the decade 1947–1956. One may be troubled, however, by data that indicate that in the period 1950–1951 the number of beds increased by 36,000 and assets rose by $35,000,000 while in 1951–1952 the number of beds increased by 20,000 and assets rose by $326,000,000. (The data in Table 3.5 include nonprofit and proprietary hospitals. These, however, represent only a small percentage of the total assets.)

3. Already included in our earlier data were expenditures in the District of Columbia. These expenditures, though by the Federal government, were included in Table 3.1.

4. The same reasoning used in the latter point can, however, be applied to hospital care, too. Just as levels of pensions are set by legislative action so, too, are expenditures on hospital care.

5. Some, at least, could theoretically be obtained, but a separate research project would be necessary to derive each of them.

6. A colleague has suggested that one could, with justification, include the cost of recreation, vacations, books, concerts, parks, dances, sports, and so forth, since they contribute to mental health. If carried to its logical conclusion one could include the cost of everything, i.e., the entire net national product. Such a course, while not particularly rewarding, would solve all measurement and definitional problems. It is doubtful whether it is useful, though it is convenient, to solve problems by assuming them away.

7. Even at governmental levels the data are not always segregated in a way that would permit accurate estimates about particular items. Budget items like "health" or "hospitals" include many things in addition to mental health or mental hospitals. Since government data are collected for other purposes one can regret but not be too critical regarding the lack of refinement. It is always difficult to use data which are gathered for different purposes. This problem has been, and will continue to be, one of the major problems in statistical research. This is what makes research difficult and also what makes it interesting.

8. From the point of view of society, interested in mental illness only, the costs of these nonmental illness conditions should be deducted in any case. It makes no difference who would have "paid the bill" if the individual had not been mentally ill. The cost of repairing bad teeth is simply the cost of repairing bad teeth, not the cost of mental illness. Should it be suggested, however, that by this approach the bulk of the cost of mental hospitals would be ignored, e.g., food, fuel, light, etc., we would hasten to point out that in 1954 the "salaries and wages" component of State maintenance expenditures in public prolonged-care hospitals (a component the bulk of which is clearly attributable to mental illness and only to mental illness) was 374 million or 66 per cent of total maintenance expenses.

CHAPTER IV

1. We assume individuals over age seventy are retired. Should the reader disagree, he can select any higher age he desires. The illustration would still be valid.

2. "In general, the labor force consists of all persons who, during a specific calendar week, have jobs or are seeking jobs (U.S. Bureau of the Census, 1953, p. 1A-5)."

3. It is probable that the relatively low incidence of mental illness in the older age groups, as reported in the survey, is accounted for by the fact that older individuals did not return to their jobs. The survey dealt with *absence,* i.e., with illness-absenteeism.

4. The approach used follows in large measure that of Reynolds, 1956.

5. The earlier approach said that the loss was equal to the entire working years expected, 39, 37, 29, 21, 13, 6, 1 for the various age groups; our adjustment changes these losses to 12, 10, 10, 9, 7, 4, 1 for the same groups.

6. The reader may wonder why our estimate, which runs about $160 million, is so much lower than the estimate of $2,061,526,350 (Nat. Committee Against Mental Illness, Inc., 1957, p. 12). There are a number of reasons, some more significant than others. Our estimate is based on 118,609 first admissions to public prolonged-care hospitals; that of the National Committee is based on 443,-339 new *and* returned patients admitted to mental hospitals and psychiatric units of general hospitals. This, of course, accounts for only a small part of the difference since our estimates are 8 per cent of the National Committee estimates while our admissions are 27 per cent. Even if we used 443,339 patients as our base, our losses would be only $590 million. A second reason for the differences is that we deal with 1952 wage and salary income (male and female) as opposed to 1955 money income. The major reason for the differences is, however, that the National Committee estimates assume that every admission, man, woman, child, or aged would have earned the average money income of $4650 per spending unit (a spending unit is any *group* of people living together and

pooling its income for general spending purposes). It is hard to defend a position that suggests that every member of a group earns an amount equal to the total income of that group. Even if the National Committee estimate were reduced somewhat by using the lower average income for wage earners figure, it is difficult to see how we can impute this wage to *all* admissions since many in this group are known not to be wage earners (women, children, retired people, etc.). The real differences between the two estimates lie in the fact that the larger estimate uses an income figure that is too large and imputes this figure to all first admissions (the same type of error is made when the Committee estimates the loss in Federal income taxes). In our estimate the loss in income is imputed *only* to those who would have earned that income.

CHAPTER VII

1. The reader will notice the word "direct" in this sentence. It is only direct costs that can be eliminated. This is a point to which we shall return later.

2. In a letter dated March 10, 1958, Dr. Paul H. Hoch, New York, State Commissioner of Mental Hygiene, described the basis of these calculated savings:

"These savings are not due solely to reductions of 450 and 470 patients in the respective years mentioned but to the overcoming of the normal increase in population as well. Thus, the savings in 1955–1956 would be on a potential 2,850 patients and in 1956–1957 it would be on a potential 3,320 patients.

"The estimate of $10,000,000 savings annually by 1959 was based upon a calculation of the difference between the actual costs of maintenance of the patients in the hospitals and the costs that would have been incurred had the trend of an increase of 2,400 patients a year been continued.

"The estimated savings in construction costs was based upon the assumption that for every increase of 2,400–3,000 patients, the equivalent of a new additional institution would be necessary. At the cost of construction which has prevailed recently, approxi-

mately $14,000 per bed, including utilities and the capital invest-
ment required by the additional population, would have been in
the neighborhood of $170 million."

3. It should be clear that an extension of life expectancy does
not alter the indirect costs since, under present work standards,
the extension of years of life occur at a time when the individual
is retired. The average age of death is already beyond the average
age of retirement.

References

Administrator of Veterans Affairs, 1957. *Annual Report, 1956.* Government Printing Office.

Albee, G., and Dickcy, Marguerite, 1957. Manpower trends in three mental health professions. *Am. Psychologist, 12:* 57.

American Medical Association, 1956. *American Medical Directory.*

Applegate, C., 1954. Annual per capita operating costs and other indices of level of service. *Proceedings of the Third Conference of Mental Health Administrators and Statisticians.* U.S. Department of Health, Education, and Welfare, 123.

Blain, D., 1953. Survey of Extent and Distribution of Psychiatric Skill and Experience in the United States and Canada. *Amer. J. Psychiat., 109:* 783.

Budget of the U.S. Government for Year ending June 30, 1958. Government Printing Office.

Committee on Interstate and Foreign Commerce, 1953. *Health Inquiry.* Government Printing Office, p. 1029.

Croatman, W., 1957[a]. Are you better off than the typical G.P.? *Medical Economics, 34* (no. 4) : 246.

——, 1957[b]. How the specialties compare financially. *Medical Economics, 34* (no. 5) : 115.

Dublin, L., and Lotka, A., 1946. *The Money Value of a Man.* Ronald Press.

Federal Security Agency, 1953. *Proceedings of the Second Conference of Mental Health Administrators and Statisticians.* Government Printing Office.

Ginzberg, E., 1953. Health, medicine, and economic welfare. *J. Mount Sinai Hospital, 19: 734.*

Harriman, A., 1958. Annual Message to the Legislature.

Hospitals, Administrator's Guide Issue, 1955. American Hospital Association, *29.*

Hospitals, Administrator's Guide Issue, 1957. American Hospital Association, *31.*

Interstate Clearing House on Mental Health, Council of State Governments, 1956. *Selected Tables on Resident Population, Finances and Personnel in State Mental Health Programs.*

Malzberg, B., 1950. Mental illness and the economic value of a man. *Mental Hygiene, 34:* 582.

———, 1956. Cohort studies of mental disease in New York State, 1943 to 1949. *Mental Hygiene, 40:* 450.

National Committee Against Mental Illness, Inc., 1957. *What Are the Facts about Mental Illness?*

Pollock, H., 1929. Economic loss on account of hospital cases of mental disease and associated physical disorders in New York State, 1928. *Psychiatric Quart., 3:* 186.

———, 1941. *Mental Disease and Social Welfare.* New York State Hospitals Press.

President's Commission on the Health Needs of the Nation, 1952. *Building America's Health.* Government Printing Office. Vols. 1–5.

Research Council for Economic Security, 1957. *Prolonged Illness-Absenteeism.*

Reynolds, D., 1956. The cost of road accidents. *J. Royal Statistical Society, 119:* 393.

U.S. Bureau of the Census, 1953. *U.S. Census of Population: 1950,* Vol. IV, Special Reports, Part I, Chap. A, Employment and personal characteristics. Government Printing Office.

———, 1954. *Statistical Abstract of the United States: 1954.* Government Printing Office.

U.S. Department of Health, Education, and Welfare, 1956. *Patients in Mental Institutions, 1952.* Government Printing Office.

———, 1957. *Patients in Mental Institutions, 1954.* Government Printing Office.

———, 1953. *Proceedings of the First Conference of Mental Health Administrators and Statisticians, 1951.* Government Printing Office.

U.S. Public Health Service, 1952. Maintenance expenditures in public mental hospitals. *Public Health Reports, 67:* 681.

Appendix

Joint Commission
on Mental Illness and Health

PARTICIPATING ORGANIZATIONS

American Academy of Neurology

American Academy of Pediatrics

American Association for the Advancement of Science

American Association of Mental Deficiency

American Association of Psychiatric Clinics for Children

American College of Chest Physicians

American Hospital Association

American Legion

American Medical Association

American Nurses Association and The National League for Nursing (Coordinating Council of)

American Occupational Therapy Association

American Orthopsychiatric Association

American Personnel and Guidance Association

American Psychiatric Association

American Psychoanalytic Association

American Psychological Association

American Public Health Association

American Public Welfare Association

Association for Physical and Mental Rehabilitation

Association of American Medical Colleges

Association of State and Territorial Health Officers

Catholic Hospital Association

Central Inspection Board, American Psychiatric Association

Children's Bureau, Dept. of Health, Education and Welfare

Council of State Governments

Department of Defense, U.S.A.

National Association for Mental Health

National Association of Social Workers

National Committee Against Mental Illness

National Education Association

National Institute of Mental Health

National Medical Association

National Rehabilitation Association

Office of Vocational Rehabilitation, Department of Health, Education and Welfare

United States Department of Justice

Veterans Administration

MEMBERS

Kenneth E. Appel, M.D.
Philadelphia, Pa.

Walter H. Baer, M.D.
Peoria, Illinois

Leo H. Bartemeier, M.D.
Baltimore, Maryland

Walter E. Barton, M.D.
Boston, Massachusetts

Otto L. Bettag, M.D.
Springfield, Illinois

Mr. George Bingaman
Purcell, Oklahoma

Kathleen Black, R.N.
New York, New York

Daniel Blain, M.D.
Washington, D.C.

Francis J. Braceland, M.D.
Hartford, Connecticut

Hugh T. Carmichael, M.D.
Chicago, Illinois

J. Frank Casey, M.D.
Washington, D.C.

James M. Cunningham, M.D.
Dayton, Ohio

John E. Davis, Sc.D.
Rehoboth Beach, Delaware

Neil A. Dayton, M.D.
Mansfield Depot, Conn.

Miss Loula Dunn
Chicago, Illinois

Howard D. Fabing, M.D.
Cincinnati, Ohio

Rev. Patrick J. Frawley, Ph.D.
New York, New York

Mr. Mike Gorman
Washington, D.C.

Ernest M. Gruenberg, M.D.
New York, New York

Robert T. Hewitt, M.D.
Bethesda, Maryland

Herman E. Hilleboe, M.D.
Albany, New York

Nicholas Hobbs, Ph.D.
Nashville, Tennessee

Bartholomew W. Hogan, Rear
Adm. M.C., U.S.N., Washington, D.C.

Louis Jacobs, M.D.
Washington, D.C.

M. Ralph Kaufman, M.D.
New York, New York

William S. Langford, M.D.
New York, New York

Miss Madeleine Lay
New York, New York

Ernst Mayr, Ph.D.
Cambridge, Mass.

Robert T. Morse, M.D.
Washington, D.C.

Russell A. Nelson, M.D.
Baltimore, Maryland

Ralph H. Ojemann, Ph.D.
Iowa City, Iowa

Winfred Overholser, M.D.
Washington, D.C.

Howard W. Potter, M.D.
New York, New York

Mr. Charles Schlaifer
New York, New York

Lauren H. Smith, M.D.
Philadelphia, Pa.

M. Brewster Smith, Ph.D.
New York, New York

Mr. Sidney Spector
Chicago, Illinois

Mesrop A. Tarumianz, M.D.
Farnhurst, Delaware

David W. Tiedman, Ed.D.
Cambridge, Mass.

Harvey J. Tompkins, M.D.
New York, New York

Beatrice D. Wade, O.T.R.
Chicago, Illinois

Mr. E. B. Whitten
Washington, D.C.

Helen Witmer, Ph.D.
Washington, D.C.

Luther E. Woodward, Ph.D.
New York, New York

OFFICERS

President: Kenneth E. Appel, M.D.
  Philadelphia, Pa.
Chairman, Board of Trustees: Leo H. Bartemeier, M.D.
  Baltimore, Md.
Vice-President: M. Brewster Smith, Ph.D.
  New York, N.Y.
Secretary-Treasurer: Mr. Charles Schlaifer
  New York, N.Y.
Vice-Chairman, Board of Trustees: Nicholas Hobbs, Ph.D.
  Nashville, Tenn.

STAFF

Director: Jack R. Ewalt, M.D.
  Boston, Mass.
Consultant for Scientific Studies: Fillmore H. Sanford, Ph.D.
  Austin, Texas.
Consultant in Social Sciences: Gordon W. Blackwell, Ph.D.
  Chapel Hill, North Carolina
Consultant in Epidemiology: John E. Gordon, M.D.
  Boston, Mass.
Associate Director for Administration: Richard J. Plunkett, M.D.
  Boston, Mass.
Director of Information: Greer Williams
  Boston, Mass.
Associate Director and Consultant on Law: Charles S. Brewton, LL.B.
  Boston, Mass.
Librarian: Mary R. Strovink
  Boston, Mass.

Index